Don't dare even crack the cover of for Anita Lustrea's in-your-face hon and you'll be glad she doesn't.

JERRY B. JENKINS
novelist

We have so many things to say but lack the courage because we convince ourselves we're the only ones. Anita Lustrea invites us to live boldly, honestly, and without fear, walking fully into the wholeness and healing God has for us. This is a book women can't afford to miss.

MARGARET FEINBERG
author of *The Organic God* and *Scouting the Divine*

Every woman and man needs to read Anita's passionate call to real community: no secrets, felt grace, and true freedom. Is there a greater longing in the human heart? Community is possible, even in fast-paced lives. Anita shows the way by telling her story authentically.

LARRY CRABB
New Way Ministries

What Women Tell Me reveals the authentic stories of Christian women who have tried to follow biblical truth and make difficult choices for their families and for themselves in the middle of complex situations. Anita Lustrea does not gloss over the tough issues. This book is honest, relevant, well-written, and heart-wrenching. Whether you are a woman living in the middle of a multifaceted challenge or a woman who mentors others, this book is for you!

CAROL KENT
speaker and author of *Between a Rock and a Grace Place*

Confession: I began reading Anita's book as a way of knocking one more item off my long to-do list. I intended to skim, glean the big ideas, write something nice, be done with it. But I'm *in*. I love this book. I'm wiping my own tears, canceling my evening plans, thanking God for Anita's honesty and bravery, and making a list of women for whom I'll buy copies.

SHAUNA NIEQUIST
author of *Cold Tangerines* and *Bittersweet*

When light shines in secret places, hope is restored. Anita has listened to the secret stories of her listeners for years. Now she tells these stories — laced with the sharing of her very own personal secrets. As we listen to the secret stories of us all, we find healing in the dialogue.

ELISA MORGAN
speaker, publisher, and author of *FullFill*™, www.fullfill.org

Anita Lustrea is a highly skilled conversationalist and uses her gift to bring out the best in one guest after another on her daily *Midday Connection* radio broadcast. Now having encouraged others to tell their stories, she has offered readers her own with all of its peaks and valleys. What a grand job she has done. Lustrea has shown us how to take some of life's toughest blows, and through it all, keep growing in graciousness and Christian maturity.

GORDON MACDONALD
speaker and author of *A Resilient Life* and *Who Stole My Church?*

WHAT WOMEN TELL ME

FINDING FREEDOM FROM THE SECRETS WE KEEP

ANITA LUSTREA

ZONDERVAN®

ZONDERVAN.com/
AUTHORTRACKER
follow your favorite authors

ZONDERVAN

What Women Tell Me
Copyright © 2010 by Anita Lustrea

This title is also available as a Zondervan ebook. Visit www.zondervan.com/ebooks.

This title is also available in a Zondervan audio edition. Visit www.zondervan.fm.

Requests for information should be addressed to:
Zondervan, *Grand Rapids, Michigan* 49530

Library of Congress Cataloging-in-Publication Data

Lustrea, Anita.
    What women tell me : finding freedom from the secrets we keep /
Anita Lustrea.
       p. cm.
    Includes bibliographical references.
    ISBN 978-0-310-32664-9 (softcover)
    1. Christian women—Religious life. 2. Lustrea, Anita. I. Title.
    BV4527. L87 2010
    248.8'43—dc22
                                               2010034656

Published in association with Yates & Yates, www.yates2.com.

Cover design: Laura Maitner-Mason
Cover photography: Bill Tucker Studio
Interior design: Michelle Espinoza

Printed in the United States of America

10 11 12 13 14 15 /DCI/ 23 22 23 22 21 20 19 18 17 16 15 14 13 12 11 10 9 8 7 6 5 4 3 2 1

To Melinda & Lori
We're in this thing together.

CONTENTS

FOREWORD
BY DEE BRESTIN

LISTENING TO ANITA ON THE RADIO awakens something deep in your soul. You sense you could bare your soul to this wise, warm woman. You sense she really cares.

It's not an act. She really *does* care. When Moody Radio celebrated Anita's twenty-fifth anniversary with their ministry, friends lined up at the mike. Over and over, one theme prevailed. Anita has been a voice for the voiceless: for the lonely, for the abused woman, for the starving child, for the victim of racial injustice, and for the Christian woman who bears the shame of divorce, even though she fought valiantly to save her marriage.

When my husband and the father of our five children died of cancer, our youngest daughter said, "I don't really like being around people who haven't suffered." Because Anita has suffered, she understands suffering. Now, for the first time, she shares her story—a story that transformed her heart and therefore her radio ministry. As she writes:

> When I cried out to Jesus, I was a broken heap in the middle of my kitchen floor. I didn't know where to turn, and in that moment I realized that if I, the host of a radio talk show helping women change and learn and grow and go deeper with God, didn't know where to turn, we had a problem.

Anita has repeatedly taken risks, breaking down the fences

many erected to keep her in. How I loved Larry Crabb's description of her: a penned-up filly yearning for freedom. He told her it was time to leap over the fence. She has. She is, indeed, akin to a beautiful galloping horse. May her freedom set you free!

Interspersed between the pages of Anita's story are testimonies from women who identify with her pain and yearn to be free. There's a legion of hurting Christian women out there — and they've found solace in Anita.

But Anita is not only a caring but a wise friend. Jesus heard her cry and came to her rescue as the Wonderful Counselor he is. Because of her position, and because of the enormous success of *Midday Connection*, Anita has access to a continual stream of wise and caring authors, speakers, pastors, and counselors. She reads constantly, voraciously, and discerningly — and now does us the favor of recommending the cream of the crop in counsel, books, and movies. The truth will, indeed, set you free — and Anita offers it to you.

Dee Brestin
Author of *The God of All Comfort*
and *The Friendships of Women*

Introduction

FINDING FREEDOM FROM THE SECRETS WE KEEP

IN MY TEN-PLUS YEARS OF HOSTING *Midday Connection,* a live radio program heard around the country on the Moody Radio Network, countless women have opened up and shared intimate secrets with me. On one level I'm flattered to be entrusted with these stories. On the other hand, I'm saddened, as I often get the feeling that I'm the only one who has ever been entrusted with these secrets.

My interaction with these stories has changed me in every imaginable way. From the way I think about God to the way I relate to my husband, to the way I raise my son, to the way I engage as a woman in the workplace, to the way I've dealt with my divorce. As you hear my story interwoven with the comments of other women, you'll hear your story too, and I hope you will realize you're not alone. I might be the voice for other women, but your voices have helped me know I'm not alone.

Confessing secrets is rarely pretty, but always freeing. And there appears to be a need for freedom among women in the church. There is a sickness of soul, and it is epidemic. The root cause is the secrets we carry. We are bound up with our secrets—

the kind of secrets that weigh us down and keep us from being all God intended us to be.

So how do we confess and, maybe more important, *where* do we confess our secrets? If we don't answer that fundamental question, the bleeding will never stop. My overflowing inbox at *Midday Connection* tells me that confession is not happening in the local church, at least not to the extent I'd like to see. The problem doesn't lie solely with the church. We have to learn to risk in relationship, to dive more deeply into community. There is distance between those in the body of Christ. We have far too many people coexisting in the church and not enough people interacting on a deeper relational level.

I hope you'll consider getting a group of women together to read through *What Women Tell Me* and discuss the issues presented. As you begin to share your secrets with one another, you will deepen your relationships and build trust. Some caution must be present as you put a group together, however. Not all small groups are created equal, and not all small groups are safe places to share the deepest hurts we've experienced. In chapter 1 I give guidelines for forming a safe group. If you are unable to join or gather a group like this, please use the discussion questions as personal reflection questions instead. The deeper issues that women deal with — that you are probably dealing with — need extra time for reflection and journaling.

As a woman, I saw modeled at home and at church how to keep quiet, how to sweep the truth under the rug. I learned how to apply a Band-Aid, and I nearly hemorrhaged to death because surgery was what was needed. I didn't learn how to ask for help, and I certainly didn't learn how to tell the truth about what was really going wrong. I learned how to "make nice" and "keep the peace."

I've spent my lifetime unlearning that message. When I

cried out to Jesus, I was a broken heap in the middle of my kitchen floor. I didn't know where to turn, and in that moment I realized that if I, the host of a radio talk show helping women change and learn and grow and go deeper with God, didn't know where to turn, we had a problem.

I'd been telling women to turn to Jesus, but in my moment of need I wasn't sure he'd meet me there. I prayed the prayer I'd learned from Larry Crabb: "Lord, I know you're all that I have, but I don't know you well enough for you to be all that I need." God answered my prayer and met me in the middle of my mess and helped me learn how to speak up, confront, bind up the wounded, including myself, and develop a community around me that is safe, where I can speak my mind and share how I *truly* feel. I've seen the importance of that group, that community, in helping me figure out *what* I'm feeling, even when I don't know myself. I've grown up into an adult, even though I've been of adult age for many years. And I finally learned, as an adult, the value of female friendships and the richness they bring to life.

I've been in Christian radio for over twenty-five years now, and I've been singing and speaking to women for even longer. I've been a follower of Christ for over forty years. I've been taught theology in church, in Sunday school, vacation Bible school, youth group, and Bible college. But it meant nothing until life served up situations where I had to discover what I really believed about God. I've surrounded myself with good people who have good theology, but at the end of the day, it's *my* theology that I have to hold on to. *My* beliefs about God will carry me through or leave me wanting. In the thick of things, we discover what stuck when we were sitting in those classrooms, what we truly digested and claimed as our own.

The process of growth for me has been filled with pauses and spurts. I suppose it's like that for many believers. Important things take a long time to learn. It's taken me twenty-five years to find and develop my voice, and the greater part of those twenty-five years to come to a place of wholeness. I wouldn't be so bold as to say that I have *something* to say, but I definitely have something I feel *compelled* to say.

I enter into this book with a measure of fear. When one speaks the truth, usually some are offended. One of the biggest fears for a woman is loss of relationship, and I've learned that when I speak my voice, sometimes loss of relationship occurs. But I desperately want to see women walk into the fullness of who God created them to be, to walk in freedom. I want them to live out the truth and spirit of Galatians 5:1: "It is for freedom that Christ has set us free. Stand firm, then, and do not let yourselves be burdened again by a yoke of slavery." God's grace must rule the day. Speaking that message is worth all the risk!

As you read this book, it is my desire to help free you from the overwhelming message that, as a woman, you are not enough — not strong enough, not beautiful enough, not thin enough, not whole enough. The truth is, none of us is "enough"; that's where Christ comes in. That is the very first message of freedom I want you to hear. You may have been physically or emotionally abused, your self-esteem may have been decimated by a husband, you may be so lonely you think you are going to die, or maybe you believe that for some reason God has sidelined you from serving him. Whatever wounds you are carrying that make you feel that you are "not enough," Satan will use those as part of his strategy to sideline you from being all that God intended.

Jesus is the starting and the ending place in this book. Jesus is the lover and the healer of a woman's soul. If we believe that, it will change the way we see ourselves, our sisters, our mothers, and our daughters. And it will change the way we relate to our husbands and brothers, our fathers and sons.

Please journey together with me as I share snippets of stories from women who have touched me and as I tell my own story. Risk opening your heart to Jesus, and watch the healing begin.

chapter one

IT'S LONELY AT CHURCH

What Women Tell Me:
> *When I enter my church I feel lonely. I some-times feel like I should go somewhere else.*

•••

I SAW THE CRUMPLED PIECE OF paper out of the corner of my eye as I stood talking to an acquaintance at the end of choir rehearsal. I didn't think much of it, but my compulsivity kicked in and I couldn't leave it there on the floor. I finished my conversation, bent over, and picked up the paper to toss it in the wastebasket. At the last second I decided to uncrumple and read it. I saw my handwriting, and my heart sank.

I headed into the choir room as usual that Wednesday night anticipating an evening of worshiping God through music. You see, I love to sing. I spent the greater part of my life singing with my family in concerts or in the car, traveling with choirs or small contemporary singing groups, or performing solo concerts. In my midtwenties through my early thirties, I pursued a career in music, but with the birth of my son I pulled back the reins on my singing and settled into full-time employment with Moody Radio. Singing in the choir fed my soul. So the choir room was a sacred space to me. Lifting my voice with the fifty other voices in the choir was something I'd do five nights a week if everyone else would show up.

Our choir director usually started us off with vocal warmups and then had us rehearse a few anthems before taking a break for a devotional time. We always exchanged prayer requests at the end of that break. We wrote them down and put them in a basket as it passed, then took one from the basket as it made its way back around.

This evening was different. Our choir director asked us to write down a personal prayer request, something that was really weighing on our hearts that we might not otherwise share publicly. Then he challenged us to sign our names if we felt we could. It didn't take long to write my request. I was surprised at how easily the words flowed from my pen. I'd written a very personal request but couldn't decide if I would sign my name. I sat there fondling my piece of paper, waiting, watching the basket get closer. With palms sweating, at the last second, I signed my name, folded the piece of paper, and tossed it in the passing basket. I had taken a huge risk that night in deciding to bare my soul. I remember thinking, "Anita, you are really desperate to do this." I was.

Now as I was leaving to go home, I picked up that crumpled piece of paper to discover my own handwriting. I smoothed out the piece of paper and read it again. "I am very lonely. Please pray for me." That was my prayer request, discarded and tossed on the floor. I had taken such a risk in being vulnerable, and then to find my request crumpled up on the floor—I was devastated. I put the smoothed-out piece of paper in my Bible. I thought, "I'll take this home and throw it out myself! I'll make sure no one else can find my confession." A little piece of my heart was inked onto that piece of paper. And a little piece of me withered and died that night.

How could someone read my request and decide to throw it away? I felt like I had been discarded along with the crumpled piece of paper. Then my mind went into overdrive. "How many people saw this same piece of paper, picked it up, read it, and dropped it back on the floor?" You know how a mind works. Yours works the same way. End result: I wanted to crawl into a hole and die. I wanted to leave the choir and the church and never come back.

If you worked with me, went to church with me, lived next door to me, you had no idea the depth of my loneliness. I don't think I fully did. I was a worship leader at church, in a leadership role at work, but I was dying on the inside. I had plenty of acquaintances, but no deep experience of friendship. From what *Midday* listeners tell me, many share the same experience. I was desperately lonely in a very lonely marriage.

A few weeks later the woman who had picked my prayer request out of the basket privately identified herself and apologized. She had intended to bring a friend and come visit me, but just hadn't been able to find the time. Which is to say she'd never stopped by—or called. As she was telling me this, I remember screaming inside my head, "I can't believe you didn't hear the desperation in those words. I can't believe you are standing there telling me that you *almost* came to visit me; that you *almost* brought a friend with you, but that you didn't have time. I'm dying here. I was desperate enough to write this request and sign my name to it; can you honestly not see how lonely I am right now?" Of course that's not what I said. I kept a demure smile on my face and politely nodded assent as if I understood her intention.

When the brief conversation ended, my questions turned toward God: "Lord, where are you? Do you see me? Do you hear me? Do you care about me? Could you not send one person in this church to meet me in my loneliness? Didn't I take a risk and do my part?"

When I was in the middle of my deepest time of loneliness, I didn't have the capacity to ask some important questions. I didn't see how isolated my life had become, or how and why it had become that way.

LIVING IN ISOLATION

There are many reasons people live in isolation. About forty-four million Americans move in any given year; that's roughly 17 percent of the population. Most disorders treated by therapists are relational, and many have to do with the fact that people have lost their relational networks. Sometimes that's due to moving, sometimes due to divorce or widowhood, sometimes both. It's not unusual to have families like mine. I live in Illinois. One of my brothers lives in Maine, and one in West Virginia, with my parents residing in Florida most of the year. Many people no longer live near nuclear family. Running across the street or down the block to visit grandparents or aunts and uncles has long been a dream of mine, but never a reality. Today, we have to create family another way.

For some women the isolation is imposed on them; for many it is self-imposed. Many people want relationships and don't know how to open themselves to real community. As one *Midday Connection* listener said, "I'm so lonesome for a deep friendship with other women, but I don't know where to start."

I sense that loneliness is epidemic among women, especially Christian women, even those who go to church every Sunday. As another woman wrote, "I feel an excruciating loneliness in the midst of other Christians at church and during the home Bible study I attend."

BORN FOR RELATIONSHIP

There is a good reason why we desire relationship — because we are born to live in community. In the Genesis account of creation, we read all about God creating the heavens and the earth. We read about God creating light and separating the light from darkness, and creating sea and sky and all kinds of living creatures. But in Genesis 1:26 we are introduced to a new thought. We hear God use the pronoun *us*. "Let us make human beings in our image, in our likeness" (TNIV). It is our first clue that God exists in community: Father, Son, and Holy Spirit. We were made in the image of a Trinitarian God. We are created for, born for, relationship.

Unfortunately, by chapter 4 of the Bible things had gone horribly awry. Cain killed Abel. The small community that existed at that time was diminished by one. Cain felt pain, and whether he knew it or not, he sent himself into isolation by the death of his brother. How often have we reduced the size of our community by emotionally injuring someone to move them out of our lives or to create distance?

Fast-forward to the New Testament. God plans to deal with his sinful creation. The plan is Jesus. Jesus came to earth to be among us: Emmanuel, "God with us." Jesus could have lived on this earth, kept his distance from people, and done everything himself, but that's not what he chose to do or how he chose to live. He modeled community by choosing disciples who walked with him. A group of bumbling fishermen, tax collectors, and women followed him everywhere during his earthly ministry. Over the course of time and as relationships developed and deepened, three of the disciples became an inner circle to Jesus. These three saw him at his glory, the Transfiguration, and in his despair, Gethsemane.

We read in 1 Corinthians 12 how we, as the church, are mysteriously the body of Christ, members of each other: "A body, though one, has many parts, but all its many parts form one body.... God has put the body together, giving greater honor to the parts that lacked it, so that there should be no division in the body, but that its parts should have equal concern for each other. If one part suffers, every part suffers with it; if one part is honored, every part rejoices with it. Now you are the body of Christ, and each one of you is a part of it" (vv. 12, 24–27 TNIV). Simply put, we need each other; that's how God designed it!

Sometimes we think it's just us; we're the weak one. Only *we* need community. Once Jesus ascended to the Father, the apostles themselves realized they needed community. Surely if Jesus didn't go it alone, neither could the apostles. In Acts 12:12, once Peter had escaped from prison with the help of an angel, he headed straight to the house of Mary, the mother of John Mark, where many people had gathered to pray. He didn't go hide out somewhere; he headed toward a home where he knew the church community would be gathering. He needed the body of Christ.

The apostle Paul, in Acts 16, headed to Philippi. On the Sabbath he and his companions "went outside the city gate to the river, where we expected to find a place of prayer" (v. 13 TNIV). Paul headed to the location where he knew he would find a community of believers, or at least the possibility of finding a group. There he spoke to the gathered women, including Lydia, "a worshiper of God. The Lord opened her heart to respond to Paul's message" (v. 14 TNIV). She invited Paul and his companions to her house to stay after she and the members of her household were baptized. Paul and Silas continued ministering in the area and were thrown into jail after Paul cast an evil spirit out of a woman. You know the story. The short version of the story is they were released from prison—by an earthquake. Did they just continue on their way? No. They headed back to Lydia's, where a growing group of believers was meeting. They benefited from that community, and they in turn encouraged the gathered believers before they left town.

Some of these biblical examples are truly what we want the church to look like today: where we gather regularly to meet in community, can't live without one another, and are always looking to encourage each other. Sometimes, though, we have a naive view of community. On one hand, we envision it as folks standing around a campfire holding hands and singing "Kumbaya." But on the other hand, there is the reality of Judas's betrayal of Jesus and the three disciples falling asleep in the Garden of Gethsemane, not to mention Peter's infamous triple denial of Christ before the rooster crowed. And then there is my story. There is the excruciating reality of my loneliness even in the midst of a fifty-voice choir that met together and prayed together week in and week out. In my life the church was not functioning as true community.

One day on *Midday Connection* our guest Dannah Gresh focused on authenticity and how to support each other in healthy Christian community. Dannah wrote *The Secret of the Lord*, a book that isn't fully explained by its title. Gresh explains that "the secret of the Lord" is a rich phrase taken from Psalm 25:14 that you can't fully understand until you delve into the Hebrew text. "Its most literal translation would be the people of God who are friends." The kind of friendship Dannah is talking about is "a tight-knit group of intimate friends with unconditional trust; a circle of friends among whom weaknesses, strengths, successes, and failures are shared. Within this circle, our sins are confessed and forgiven. Our masks of perfection are removed. We aren't afraid to tell our stories, and we are truly known. The secret of the Lord is the intimate friendship that exists between believers."[1]

In that hour-long program, we offered ten books each to ten different women who would commit to forming a small group to go through the book. The book contains an interactive experience at the end of each chapter called "It's Your Turn," which lends itself to group discussion. Our goal was to help women start forming community. We wanted the leaders of the groups to report back to us about how things were going, and we hoped winning the ten books would make it easier for a woman to make phone calls and be intentional about inviting other women into community.

We got our ten volunteers. But the email response — from hundreds of women — revealed deeper issues. After I'd read the first ten or so, I saw the pattern. Almost without fail the emails read, "I am very lonely. I want to be in a small group, or find community, but I'm afraid to risk it." Some went on to say they'd been burned in the past and were hesitant to try again.

I think we need to take a look at why building community is so difficult. I believe sometimes the issue is related to spiritual warfare. We are in a spiritual battle, but we forget that we are.

SPIRITUAL WARFARE

One year I taught an adult Sunday school class during the Christmas season. And the more I studied the Incarnation, the more I thought about spiritual warfare. In the lesson I taught, I called Jesus' coming to earth an act of war. Think about it. As soon as Christ arrived on the scene, Satan tried to snuff him out.

We are in a battle, and Satan desperately wants to keep us from building relationships that will fortify our faith and strengthen us spiritually. If he can keep community from being built, he will have succeeded.

J. R. R. Tolkien's the Lord of the Rings trilogy is full of spiritual truths. My husband, son, and I watch the film version of it annually. In the first movie, *The Fellowship of the Ring*, all of the representatives of the different people groups of Middle Earth gather to discuss the fate of the ring, an evil, magical gold band that possesses whoever owns it. The Middle Earth Council decides that the ring must be destroyed by being thrown into the fires of Orodruin, the fiery mountain. All of the warriors are yelling and fighting over who will carry the ring, how dangerous the mission is, and how impossible it is.

In the middle of the din, a small voice says, "I will do it. I will carry the ring." He repeats it, trying to be heard above the others. "I will do it. I will carry the ring." Little Frodo Baggins, half the size of all but the dwarf Gimli, steps forward to volunteer for the perilous task.

Here's the important point: Frodo doesn't head out alone carrying the ring. He is surrounded, not by masses of people, but by some select friends who essentially commit to three things: to walk with him, to watch his back, and to fight off the enemy. That's what I'm talking about when I say community. I think that's the support we're lonely for.

Since the Garden of Eden the enemy has relied on one strategy. His goal is to divide and conquer. His plan is to isolate us and take us out of commission. If we are sidelined, we are of no value to the kingdom of God. I've been a pastor's wife for about five years now. One thing I've noticed is that the well of relational difficulties never runs dry. Satan has a huge bag of tricks, and he is not afraid of attacking any of God's people.

When I was dating my husband, he was running a singles ministry. As with any big ministry, there were people who were known to be gossipers. To protect ourselves, we would do most of our dating away from our home area and out of the church public's eye. We'd go to street fairs in various suburbs, or go downtown to the lakefront. We did anything and everything to avoid being fodder in the rumor mill. Gossip still traveled, but we ignored it and didn't fan the flame. When we give in and listen to these voices that are doing the work of the Evil One through gossiping, we lend credence to their message.

In my old neighborhood a petite Italian woman lived right across the street from me. The day my family moved into our home, I stepped across the street to say hello and introduce myself. There was a man out mowing the lawn and I assumed he lived there. I learned he just worked for the lawn maintenance service, but he would tell the lady of the house I had stopped by. On the following Saturday as I was out in my garage unpacking boxes and cleaning, I heard footsteps. I looked up to see my sweet neighbor coming up my driveway carrying a silver tea service and bringing me tea and cookies.

In her thick Italian accent she told me she was so sorry that she missed me when I stopped by to say hello, and then she told me that I was the first person in the neighborhood to speak to her in eighteen years. I thought surely she was wrong. Why would that be the case? As I met other neighbors, I asked what they knew about the little Italian lady. Slowly the story came out that they believed her husband was part of the Chicago mob. They told a story about someone driving down the street and throwing a Molotov cocktail through their front window and speeding away. As I inquired further, no one had actually seen that happen; they were just repeating a story that another neighbor told them. I still don't know if there was any truth to the rumor. I figured that the greater part of the story had been gossip that had kept this neighbor isolated for eighteen years. That's what sin will do.

Satan often plays with us emotionally. I'm sure we can all recount a time when we took insult when none was intended. We blow slights way out of proportion. As I have distance from my own choir room experience, I can see clearly that the woman who had my prayer request was not ill intentioned. She didn't purposely decide *not* to come visit me. Life was busy. And did I mention she had four children?

Satan uses relational messes to make us do one of two things. Either we fight like mad against it, which can be exhausting and cause people to be estranged from us, or we retreat into isolation. Either way, he wins.

I am a PK, a preacher's kid. Although there were many wonderful things about being brought up as the daughter of a pastor, like playing hide-and-seek in the church building whenever I wanted, or using the church's kitchen to cook big meals when extended family came to visit, there were also many relational patterns I eventually needed to relearn. My dad attended Bible college in an era when ministerial students were taught to maintain a distance from their congregants and not to have close friends among their parishioners so that the congregation could view you as the leader and put you on a pedestal. This put the pastor and his wife in a difficult and isolated position of trying to figure out where to find friends, and often deciding to go without. Unfortunately, this school of thinking trickled down to me. Because neither of my parents had close friends, I believed I couldn't have close friends in the church either.

Here is how this teaching played out in my life. My father was the sole pastor of small rural or inner-city churches. He was always the expert, the answer man. I saw the pressure that put on him, and when my brothers got into some trouble in high school, even though the trouble was not that big of a deal, we didn't talk about it to anyone. My mother sat in the front pew, played the piano, and smiled; she encouraged the women of the congregation, but I never sensed that she shared her greatest joys or sorrows. In fact, I never saw much range of emotion in either of my parents. I understood that to mean that it's not okay to feel, that highs and lows are unacceptable, that we have to be even-keeled and mostly on the generally pleasant, happy side of the emotional continuum.

I remember my mom talking to me about emotional, gossipy women and how I wasn't to be like those kinds of women. I understood that gossiping was sin, but I never understood what was wrong with emotion. Still, I adhered to her advice to "never let them see you cry." In fact, before I got married my mom said, "There's nothing worse than a blatting bride. Don't go down the aisle crying." So I walked down the aisle with a smile pasted on. I doubt it was my mother's intent to keep me emotionless, but as she lived out of her own woundedness as it related to not expressing feelings, I followed suit.

I never saw modeled for me how to develop a close, intimate, give-and-take friendship. The message I took in was I'd better have it all together or at least look like I have it all together, because that's what Christians do. We smile.

But I've found that people who always smile can be just as lonely as those who never smile.

Have you ever struggled with sadness, pain, or depression, but tried desperately to make your friends think everything was okay? Believing that everything is all right in others' lives and that you are the only one with problems is such a common theme in relationships. If we only knew the truth. The prevailing belief is that we would not be accepted if people really knew us, knew us at our core, and so we do whatever we can to keep up appearances. I believe we, in the church, know the language of community and have a desperate desire for it, but we continue to keep people at arm's length. To be fully known and fully loved is one of the deepest human desires. But the *fear* of being fully known is almost equal to the *desire* to be known.

The process of trying to hide and keep up appearances is exhausting. Have you ever played with a beach ball in a pool, trying to keep it hidden under water? It takes a lot of hard work to keep it concealed below the surface of the water. I've tried to sit on a beach ball in a pool, and it takes a tremendous amount of balance to keep from falling off and having it pop up to the surface. Once it comes to the surface and you're not working to push it down under, all your energies can be used elsewhere. When all our energies are being used to hide, conceal, and not be real, we have little energy left for anything else, especially building satisfying relationships.

When I interviewed Dan Allender on his book *To Be Told*, he said that we have a picture of whom we wish to be — our *ideal self*, exhibiting a specific set of values, beliefs, and dreams. And yet we often aren't what we want to be; we end up choosing what others expect us to be — our *ought self*. The healthier we become emotionally, the more the *ideal* and the *ought* come together, forming our *real* self. I have lived many, many years out of my *ought* self.

When I was growing up, my mother would call me perfect. I remember at age five or six playing in the corner of the kitchen one day when someone was sitting at the kitchen table visiting with my mother. I'm sure the two of them didn't know I was listening, but I heard my mother say, "She's perfect. She's an angel. Sometimes I wonder if she's a dream, if she'll be gone one day when I go to her room to get her up in the morning." At the time I smiled at the words. How amazing that my mom thought that. Of course I had no idea how those words would weigh on me and play out in my life.

Fast-forward forty-four years. I was at a family celebration, a dinner at a restaurant with about eight to ten of us around a large table. I was the junior member of the group by a generation. Someone said something to my mother about how proud she must be of me hosting a radio program and writing a book. My mom immediately took off on a litany of "how perfect Anita was as a child, and really she still is." I've heard that same story over and over throughout my life. Either from the mouth of my mother or played on the tapes in my own mind.

That's a heavy mantle to put on a small child. What did I do with that label? I lived into my mother's view of me. I tried to *be* perfect. It wasn't until years later that it all came crashing down with the failure of my marriage. To be honest, it was a relief to have the perfect picture shattered.

LEARNING TO TRUST, CHOOSING TO RISK

Most of us are in positions of influence. We influence coworkers and kids, friends and fellow committee members, just to name a few. Because of the way God made us, we are in the perfect place to risk trying to reach out and build healthy, honest relationships. The pursuit of God and the pursuit of relationships with other members of Christ's body go hand in hand. The two great impulses of our souls are upward and outward. We simply reflect the design of God. So how do we grow into and through community—Christian community?

In the 1960s and 1970s when I was growing up, Christians were very private about their spiritual lives, so I didn't see those closest to me modeling openly how to deeply press into Jesus and lean on him. Maybe they did, but I didn't see it. Besides a time of family devotions, when after dinner my dad would read from a devotional book after one of us kids had read the corresponding Scripture passage, our spiritual lives were something that happened behind closed doors. We were not duplicitous in the sense that we were mean, nasty people behind closed doors and then pasted on a smile when we left the confines of home, but we were false in the sense that we didn't even share our deep loneliness and heartaches with each other inside the walls of the family home. I think my whole family was desperately lonely but didn't know how to give voice to it.

I grew up singing the old hymn "Tell It to Jesus."

> *Now are you weary, are you heavy-hearted?*
> *Tell it to Jesus,*
> *Tell it to Jesus;*
> *Are you grieving over joys departed?*
> *Tell it to Jesus alone.*
> *Tell it to Jesus,*
> *Tell it to Jesus,*
> *He is a friend that's well-known;*
> *You've no other such a friend or brother,*
> *Tell it to Jesus alone.*

I agree with half of the theology of this hymn. I needed to learn how to tell it to Jesus. But not only to Jesus. I needed to learn how to develop friendships and deepen relationships, which we'll talk about in the next chapter. You'll see some of my bumbling attempts at building relationships there. But I did need to learn how to tell it to Jesus first. And learn how to tell it to Jesus when I believed no one else understood. Jesus lived his whole earthly life misunderstood. Who else but Jesus could completely understand my life? Learning how to express my emotions was a significant breakthrough not only in strengthening relationships with friends, but in going deeper in my relationship with Jesus. We'll talk more about how that breakthrough happened a bit later.

I sense many of us struggle with deep loneliness because we don't believe we are loved daughters of God. If someone asked you if God loves you, I'm sure you'd answer yes. My guess is that deep down you don't really believe it. Because I believed that I didn't really matter, that I was unlovable, I didn't believe God would want to hear my heart poured out to him. Finally God healed me after I spent time in Scripture and looked deeply at Psalm 139, Ephesians 2:1 – 10, and the story of Hagar in Genesis 16. I saw a direct correlation to how I experienced relationships. Do you believe you can be vulnerable with God? Do you believe he hears you, or sees you, as in the case of Hagar? Are you willing to sit in God's presence and listen for his voice of love?

As we lean into God, we can ask the Spirit to help us discern to whom we should open ourselves. We may not — and maybe should not — trust everyone in our congregations. Everyone needs a friend, but not everyone is safe, especially for those of us who feel particularly fragile. Should I have expected a randomly chosen choir member to respond to my pain in any manner other than prayer and possibly a card? I'm not sure. Should I have associated finding my "confession" on the floor as a sign that I had been personally discarded? Probably not — but then you know how the mind works.

A recurring question as women attempt to find a place to trust and be trusted is, "How do I know if someone is safe? How do I know if I've entered a safe group, especially if I didn't hand-pick the participants?" Henry Cloud and John Townsend, well known for their book *Boundaries*, have a small book titled *Safe People* that I recommend. They pose the question, "Is the church safe, or is it dangerous?" The answer is, "It is both." Sometimes we are fortunate to find good relationships, and other times we run into disaster.

How can we better guard against running into disaster? Cloud and Townsend say that a safe person does three things: "1. Draws us closer to God. 2. Draws us closer to others. 3. Helps us become the real person God created us to be."[2] It takes maturity and discernment to spot safe people. Let's face it, some of us have broken "people pickers." So let me give a little more of an explanation of what a safe group might look like. A safe group will be full of grace and also laced with truth. We need to be able to speak the truth to each other, to confront when needed, but always in a loving, grace-filled, noncondemning way. A small group also needs to be present for each other in all of life's diverse circumstances, the good times and the crises.

What if, when the woman who read my prayer request approached me to confess that she meant to visit or call me, I had responded differently, more authentically? After all, she was honest with me about her intentions and apologized for not following through. Had I ever done that in my life? Let me count the ways! What if I'd said, "I'm sure you're busy, and really, I don't know what I expected to happen. I didn't really know how lonely I was until I had a moment of quiet and put my pen to paper. Maybe we can meet at Starbucks one day next week. Would that work for you?" I think both of us had been immobilized by fear. I had fear of rejection, and she had fear of what she might be signing up for.

I'll talk more about my own journey — taking the risk to be honest with friends — in chapter 2. Here I'll focus on foundational aspects of trust and community. If we are to be the body of Christ, and to experience the body of Christ as it was meant to function, then we have to become vulnerable, but not just vulnerable. We must become authentic with each other.

In Ephesians Paul spends a lot of time talking about the body of Christ and how it should work.

> Now these are the gifts Christ gave to the church: the apostles, the prophets, the evangelists, and the pastors and teachers. Their responsibility is to equip God's people to do his work and build up the church, the body of Christ. This will continue until we all come to such unity in our faith and knowledge of God's Son that we will be mature in the Lord, measuring up to the full and complete standard of Christ.
>
> Then we will no longer be immature like children. We won't be tossed and blown about by every wind of new teaching. We will not be influenced when people try to trick us with lies so clever they sound like the truth. Instead, we will speak the truth in love, growing in every way more and more like Christ, who is the head of his body, the church. He makes the whole body fit together perfectly. As each part does its own special work, it helps the other parts grow, so that the whole body is healthy and growing and full of love.
>
> Ephesians 4:11–16 NLT

Paul is giving this group of Ephesian Christians a vision for growing to maturity. He says, "We will speak the truth in love, growing in every way more and more like Christ, who is the head of his body, the church." But Paul also talks about how the body of Christ works and explains that "each part does its own special work." Every part of the body has a purpose. Thank goodness there are not fifty of me in our church. There would never be coffee and donuts on Sunday mornings, and the website wouldn't get updated very often.

I had been visited by mice in my previous house, so I set some traps. The traps worked, but I was traumatized by the sight of the mouse, still wiggling in the trap. I was alone at home one evening and didn't know what to do. I was so thankful for the body of Christ. I called friends of mine, Kim and Chris, and in no time Chris was pulling into my driveway, plastic grocery bag in hand along with a long-handled set of pliers. The mouse was taken care of because I had reached out to other members of the body and they responded. A little vulnerability on my part to admit I had mice, a little kindness on the part of Kim and Chris as I interrupted their evening. A bit of community developing and loneliness lessening.

Have you seen the movie *Freedom Writers*? It is a gripping story of inner-city high school kids who've largely been raised on violence. A young first-year English teacher comes along their freshman year and gives them what they need most, a voice of their own. This teacher gets her students to tell their own stories as they write in diaries. They also start to listen to each other's stories. What happens? They begin to form a supportive community. And when one of the students is evicted from his apartment, he finds a safe place—a home—in the unlikeliest of places: his English classroom.

This movie gives us clues on how to form a safe community. First, you need to find people you can spend time with regularly, face-to-face. Then you need to share your lives, both talking and listening, with the understanding that nothing will be repeated outside your meetings. My friend Mindy Caliguire, while on *Midday Connection*, told a story about a developing relationship when she was a young pastor's wife. She desperately needed a friend and confidant. A neighbor who finally began to open up and do some mutual sharing told Mindy something of a medium confidential nature. The next week when she and Mindy met, the friend asked, "Did you share with anyone what I told you last week?" Mindy said, "No, I wouldn't do that; you asked me to keep it in confidence." Mindy's friend said, "You passed the test. I told you something that wouldn't have been horrible if it got out, but I needed to test you to see if I could trust you with deeper confidences." Test the waters as you enter into any new relationship.

It also helps to have common goals to work toward, common projects you are part of, whether that be motherhood or a Bible study or a charity or a school board. Are you in a relationship you would label as true community? Are you in a community that draws out the best in you? A place that draws you into the arms of Jesus?

Do you have those places you go that feel like home? Are there homes of friends where when you walk in you feel known? Do you have true community in your life where you know others and they know you and you are not alone?

C. S. Lewis said it best: "[Jesus] works on us in all sorts of ways: ... through nature, through our own bodies, through books, sometimes through experiences which seem (at the time) anti-Christian. But above all, he works on us through each other. Men are mirrors, or carriers of Christ to other men. Sometimes unconscious carriers."[3] When we are in community, we are mirrors for each other. When we walk the path alone, we don't have true perspective, because God made us for community.

The night I found my crumpled prayer request on the choir room floor, I could have left the choir and never come back. I was hurt, sure, but I knew God wanted me in relationships with others, even if it meant risking again. Even in my loneliness, I knew I needed relationships. Satan would have loved for me to leave the choir and the church. He would love to isolate you and keep you separated from the body of Christ. If you are lonely in the church, are you willing to risk one more time? Success is not guaranteed. An invitation to engage with Jesus is.

DISCUSSION QUESTIONS

1. What's your experience been dealing with loneliness? Has it touched your life, or the life of a friend or family member?

2. Can loneliness ever be disguised as busyness? How and why?

3. How much of loneliness is self-created?

4. Have you ever felt lonely in the midst of a marriage or in the middle of your church congregation?

5. How can you be mindful of those around me who might be lonely?

6. How do you turn to God during seasons of loneliness?

7. The Psalms, especially the psalms of lament, can be a great comfort in times of loneliness. Read some of these psalms of lament and cry out to God through them: 12, 13, 22, 27, 38, 44, 51, 55, 69, 74, 79, 90, 109.

chapter two

BEST FRIENDS FOREVER — OR MAYBE NOT

What Women Tell Me:
I truly don't have a good friend and I'm almost fifty years old. I have been stabbed in the back, talked about, and feel what is the use?

Why is it so hard for us to connect as women? I long for someone to pick up the phone and call me to see how I am doing.

• • •

A WELL-KNOWN HARVARD MEDICAL SCHOOL NURSES' health study reported that those who had the most friends over a nine-year period cut their risk of early death by a certain percent. Just take a guess at the percent. Don't look ahead; make an honest stab at by what percent people cut their risk of early death.

Okay, here's the answer: 60 percent. That shocked me. In fact, it was determined that not having a close friend or confidant was as detrimental to someone's health as smoking or being overweight. There's more to friendship than alleviating our negative feelings of loneliness. So why don't more people invest in relationships? Maybe a few highlights of my friendship history will shed some light on the issue.

I've had more than forty years of attempted friendships. More failures than successes, it seems, but the successes are coming in greater number these days. At least I'm making positive progress. Maybe you'll spot yourself in some of these stories.

SOMEONE TO PLAY WITH

I don't really remember friends before the first grade when we moved from Maine to suburban Philadelphia. The first friends I remember are Jan and Lisa, two slightly older neighbor girls who also attended the church my dad pastored. To call them friends is a bit of an exaggeration, but they were the only girls in the whole neighborhood, and I desperately wanted someone to play with. So when they snuck cigarettes from their three-pack-a-day mother, I smoked along with them out in the woods.

There was something exciting and dangerous about the whole scenario. We lived in fear that our parents would find out, at least I did. Smoking was one of those horrible evils where, if I was caught, it would be the end of the world as I knew it.

When their mom starting yelling at Jan, Lisa, and their two other siblings about missing cigarettes, they didn't swipe any more. Our moment of living on the edge only happened three or four times. I quit hanging out with those two when I realized their mom didn't care where they were or how long they were gone. My mom always asked where I was going and how long I'd be gone, and if she thought my brothers and I had been gone too long, she rang this large, loud cowbell that could be heard all over the neighborhood. On some level, even as a child, I knew someone had my back, and it was my mom and dad. Even if I didn't know how to form friendships with good people like my parents, that's what I kept looking for.

Another childhood friend, Sally, was strong and domineering. She had an outdoor pool, so I liked to go to her house in the summer—until one day when she tried to push me down and hold me under. It seemed she was forever trying to get me to do something I didn't want to do. Nothing bad, just always doing what she wanted. Sally was a bully. We played alone, just the two of us, and she was so much stronger than me, physically and emotionally, that I felt as if I had no "out." It wasn't long before I found reasons not to play with her.

Then there was Pauline, whose family took me to expensive places. This appealed to me because my family couldn't afford it. My dad, besides being a full-time pastor, drove a school bus to bring our income up to just above the poverty level. Pauline's family often went to the opera and live theater productions and invited me along. I was flattered, but also felt somewhat uncomfortable, though I couldn't pinpoint why for a while. Pauline gave me expensive gifts, but then she expected total loyalty, what I'd call friend worship. I extricated myself from this relationship after a while too.

I often felt like a misfit. I always wore hand-me-downs from a girl at church who was a size or two bigger than me. When other girls wore skirts above their knee, I wasn't allowed. And once kids knew I was a preacher's kid, there was a certain expectation of behavior that I lived up to. I was sometimes called goody-two-shoes. On top of that, I was painfully shy. That was the exterior. On the interior I deeply desired connection with God but didn't sense that anyone else in my world wanted the same thing. I'd made a commitment to Christ when I was seven. That might seem like a young age for a child to really understand a decision like that. But I was an intense child. I loved God with everything in me and wanted to know him more deeply, and I wanted to share him with the friends in my life.

So when a new girl, Alex, showed up when I was in sixth grade, I immediately reached out to her to be her friend. I knew what it felt like to be left out and alone. Alex was probably the cutest girl in the class, and it didn't take her long to start hanging with the more popular crowd. I'm grateful that she always showed me kindness, but we grew apart because I didn't fit her image.

JUNIOR HIGH MISFIT

Then came the trauma of the junior high years. Today when I hear mothers describe their daughters' adolescent relational struggles, I cringe. Things may be harder for girls now, but even in the early seventies friendships were fraught with drama. You might say that Candy was my first BFF (best friend forever). We were inseparable. We attended the same church; we were both leaders in the youth group. We lived far enough away that we attended different elementary schools, but when we entered junior high, our schools fed into the same school. I was excited to finally be going to the same school as Candy!

We rarely had class together, but I'd catch up with Candy in the hall when I could. She introduced me to some of her friends from her elementary school, and I did the same. She was very outgoing and very well liked. At the same time, I had a growing sense that she was trying to avoid me.

That same year my brother David received his first mailing from Teen Missions International, a youth missionary organization. He had no interest, but I watched him throw out the mailing and waited until he left the house to go into his room and dig through the trash. His girlfriend had spent the previous summer in Oaxaca, Mexico, on a Teen Missions team, and when she returned, I'd never seen someone's light for Jesus shine so bright. I knew this was for me. I wanted to go.

Teen Missions had a minimum age requirement, age thirteen. At age twelve I picked the brochure out of David's trash can and pored over the different options of mission teams that Teen Missions sent out. I turned thirteen at the end of my seventh grade year, two weeks before the teams took off for the summer. I begged my parents to let me go. I don't know if I had an unusual appetite for adventure as a teen, if I wanted to get away from home for some reason, or if I just wanted to find like-minded teens. As I look back I think it was a bit of all three.

My parents promised to pray about it before giving an answer, and I drove them crazy asking if they'd reached a decision. After a month they said yes, I could go, but only if I stayed in the United States. So at age thirteen I headed out with thirty other teens to share my faith with people we encountered at many of the national parks of the West. Thank goodness for two weeks of training in evangelism before we hit the road.

This was the first for me of many Teen Missions trips. Each summer trip lasted ten weeks, with two weeks of boot camp, where teams developed a sense of unity, underwent training for their particular mission experience, and had times of worship, Bible study, and teaching. Teen Missions encompassed my entire summer. I would go, make friends with my thirty teammates, and then come home never to see them again. Have you ever had an experience with friends or coworkers where you were put in an intense situation for a short period of time? Quick friendships are forged and they go deep rather quickly because of the shared experience. But it's not the kind of deep that stands the test of time. I wonder if it's different today in the age of cell phones, email, and Facebook. As wonderful as my Teen Missions experiences were, the end-of-summer goodbyes were very painful. I actually think these short, intense relational experiences were a hindrance to building deeper friendships later on in life.

I came home after my first Teen Missions experience with several goals. I wanted to go again next summer. I wanted to persuade as many people as I could to come with me on a team next summer. I wanted to go on a special ten-day Christmas team where we would spend Christmas day on the beach. I also wanted to find a Christian high school to attend so I could have the Teen Missions experience of hanging out with like-minded kids year-round and not having to say goodbye at the end of ten weeks.

I began asking my parents if there would be any possibility that I could go to a Christian high school. I knew there wasn't one in our area, but I asked anyway. In the meantime I couldn't wait for the Christmas team. I'm surprised my parents said yes to this, since I'd miss Christmas with the family. I think my powers of persuasion, as the only daughter, were pretty strong. As I look back, it seems like I checked out of my family at around age thirteen. I lived for my Teen Missions experiences and for going to a Christian school, and that was about it. I was frustrated that no one else wanted to change the world. I had an obsession with being with like-minded Christian people.

I attended the Christmas team, and it was a pitifully small group of about eight or ten people. It was definitely a group of misfits, which is more and more how I saw myself. I wasn't a good fit for the world I was in and I didn't know what to do with that, other than try to get away from the world I was in. Christmas Day on the beach was not all it was advertised to be. I was extremely lonely in the midst of my small team, but unable to admit that to my family or myself. My mom and dad and brothers had made a trip to Florida that year for Christmas. They visited grandparents I'd seen only one other time in my life, and they took a trip to Disney World with aunts, uncles, and cousins. I still can't fully grasp why I gave that up. I didn't even feel like I fit into my own family.

I couldn't wait for the new Teen Missions brochure to come in the mail. Where could I go next summer? I dreamed of the possibilities. When the mailing arrived, the more exotic the location the better, and since my parents said I could go overseas this time, I settled on a team going to Lanzarote, one of the Canary Islands off the coast of Morocco, West Africa. My team was going to build the first evangelical church on the island. I had convinced two friends from church to go on a Teen Missions trip, including Candy, along with my brother David. None of them ended up going to Lanzarote with me, but that didn't matter. I was excited about what I knew God would do in all of our hearts over the course of the summer.

In ninth grade something happened that would mark me and change the way I developed friendships. I saw Candy at a distance talking with a group of her friends. When I came up behind her, she didn't see me. I stood there a moment listening. I was going to be funny and put my fingers up behind her head like rabbit ears, but when I heard her drop the F-bomb, I didn't know what to do or how to respond. This wasn't the Candy who had gone on a Teen Missions trip, who led youth group meetings, and who did Bible studies with me. I acted like I had just walked up and hadn't heard anything.

This discovery devastated my fourteen-year-old heart. I didn't see it at the time, but that betrayal caused me to close off parts of myself to others so I would never experience that kind of pain again. The fallout of my relationship with Candy stunted my growth in developing and deepening friendships for years to come. And it influenced the way I would relate to other women. As I cocooned my heart, no one had access beyond the surface level.

After this incident with Candy, I deepened my resolve to find a Christian school. I had this notion that if I attended one, everyone would be on the same page and I would never experience betrayal again. Also during junior high I became the leader of a group of misfits. My zeal was a little over the top. I felt it was my duty to share my relationship with Jesus with whoever would listen, so I started carrying my Bible to school and gathering a small group of disciple friends whom I could talk to (mostly talk at) about God.

To further make me a misfit, I'd wear gaudy religious jewelry. One favorite was a two-inch square pendant that had a fist imprinted on it with the words "I am a revolutionary and my hero is Jesus Christ." The other favorite, a leather pendant about three inches in diameter, featured the fish symbol and the words "Jesus Christ, God's Son, Savior." I would also wear a round button pin that read "Christianity is not a religion; it's a way of life." It's really no wonder that Candy tried to avoid me in the hallways at school.

With hindsight I see that, like most middle schoolers, I looked long and hard for a way to fit in. I wanted people around me who were like me, or whom I could help to be like me. Being religious felt the most comfortable and was all I had seen modeled. It's easy for me to see now that this was the beginning of my self-righteous attitude.

CHRISTIAN HIGH SCHOOL

With my persistence about attending a Christian school, my dad located two Christian boarding high schools as possibilities. I chose Toccoa Falls Academy in Toccoa Falls, Georgia. Following my trip to Lanzarote, I arrived home just in time to pack up and head to Georgia. I spent my sophomore year at Toccoa Falls, then took off with Teen Missions again for another ten weeks, this time to Guatemala, where we built a church for Kanjobal Indians in San Miguel Acatan, in the mountains. I met another wonderful team of teenagers only to say goodbye at the end of the summer.

This year the goodbyes were more difficult. Not only did I say goodbye to my Teen Missions team members, but Toccoa Falls Academy, after years in existence, decided to close its doors. I had opened up some of the closed-up real estate of my heart when I began attending Toccoa Falls, thinking, "Hey, I'll be here for three years and I can develop some really close friendships." The blow of the school's closing did what all my goodbyes had done the past several years: closed off my heart a little more.

My junior and senior years I attended Ben Lippen School in Asheville, North Carolina. After my junior year I once again joined Teen Missions for the summer. This time I headed with my team to Tamazunchale, Mexico, where we helped to renovate and repair a local Bible college and seminary. My husband finds it hard to believe, but at age sixteen, I was the foreman on the roofing crew that reroofed the library (after two summers on other work projects, I had more construction experience than most of the guys on the team). I also wielded a mean shovel and killed a rather large tarantula the day I was helping mix cement for a sidewalk. Again I said goodbye at the end of the summer. I was becoming an expert at knowing how to cocoon my heart.

During my senior year in high school, my dad took a new assignment at a church in Kansas City, Kansas. Since I was away at boarding school, it didn't really disrupt my life. The summer between high school and college, I moved back to my parents' house in Kansas City. For the first time in four summers, I was home and not somewhere around the globe. I got a job at a local grocery store to earn money for college—that would be Moody Bible Institute in Chicago.

COLLEGE FRIENDSHIPS AND BEYOND

At Moody, after deciding on Bible/theology as a major (mainly because I failed my theory entrance exam to the music major), I settled in and again started to open up my heart to friendships. I decided that the college experience would be long enough for me to form some deeper relationships, and that was indeed the case. I also sang with a tight-knit, eight-member group called the New Disciples. We traveled and sang and promoted the school.

I lived on the same floor in the dorm all of my years at Moody and developed some wonderful relationships that I still maintain to this day. Debby, Mary, and Judy are three friends I can pick up with anytime, anywhere. And Hannah and I were in the New Disciples and forged a wonderful relationship. I was the maid of honor in her wedding. Bill, also in the New Disciples, and I have worked together at Moody Radio for more than twenty-five years now, and are probably more like family than colleagues or friends.

After graduating from Moody, I joined a Christian singing group, the Internationals, and toured for a year: nine months in the United States and three in Europe. I was excited to spend a year singing, something I dearly loved. On the other hand, knowing that I was signing on for a one-year gig sobered me. I'd be living and traveling with five people, only to have them ripped out of my life in twelve months. I thought, "If I protect my heart and don't get close to these people, I won't experience the pain I've come to know over the past six or seven years when I have to part ways."

This seemed like wise thinking, but God didn't create us to guard our hearts from human relationships. I would ride in our bus usually reading a book or writing letters to my parents or college friends, not really engaging in conversation. A few weeks into the tour, the two other female singers, Janine and Donna, confronted me. They gently said, "What's wrong? It seems like you are holding back and not sharing part of yourself with us. If you don't open up to us, this is going to be a difficult year."

I thank God that the Holy Spirit quickened my heart and allowed me to hear their good intent. I realized what I had been trying to do. As we talked, I cried — I think we all cried. With a wall broken down, 1981–82 became a powerful year of friendship building. Not because I volunteered to step out of my comfort zone, but because Janine and Donna were willing to risk relationally with me.

FAITH AND FRIENDSHIP

Despite my foray into friendship with Janine and Donna, I still found myself continually in shallow friendships. Not because of the other person, but always because of me. I felt a certain amount of frustration, but those trying to develop a friendship with me felt it even deeper. I had a good friend, Beth, tell me that she felt there was a wall between us and that she could only get to a certain level in our friendship. She asked if I felt it, and at that point, maybe I did, but I didn't know how to do anything about it. As one listener commented, "I'm so lonesome for a deep friendship with other women, but I don't know where to start." I knew where to start, but not how to go very deep.

One of the most frequently asked questions when it comes to developing friendships is, "How do I begin?" It usually takes some relational risk. Sometimes crisis is the catalyst. That's how I "broke through" to a friendship with an across-the-street neighbor, Faith, about ten years ago. When I moved to the neighborhood, Faith and I met at the school bus stop, where we discovered our kids attended the same school. Life just happened with not a great deal of interaction the first year except for the occasional borrowing of sugar and kids playing in the backyards. Then one day crisis hit my life. I won't go into all the details, but it was the beginning of the end of my marriage.

You know what I realized? I had no close friends. I suddenly felt desperate and in a difficult situation, and desperation will drive you to do things you wouldn't ordinarily do. In this case it meant taking the huge risk of trusting someone to listen to me, to keep confidence, and to help me get through the day. I went to Faith's house and knocked on the door. She responded to my "Can I talk to you?" by opening her door and inviting me in. My marriage had just hit a semi head-on, I explained, and I needed serious help. Now that's not really how you want to start a friendship. But Faith didn't turn me away.

A couple of years later I talked to Faith about that January day when I barged into her life. I asked her if she had been longing for deeper relationships too. She said yes, but things like kids and busyness had crowded out other relationships. She didn't see friendship as a priority, but she was lonely.

You don't usually start a relationship by coming out with your deepest, darkest secrets, but desperation will break us out of our unhealthy patterns. Desperation drove me to open up a dialogue with Faith. But solid friendships are not forged overnight. Friendships take time to grow. Faith and I logged many hours walking around a block or two or three after our kids got on the school bus in the morning.

The beginning of a friendship can be less dramatic and start with small risks. Asking someone for coffee or talking about your children's antics can be a start. When I started singing on a praise team at church, I sat next to Sandy in rehearsal each week. At first we made small talk. We already knew we had a mutual love of music, and then we discovered our sons were in the same Sunday school class at church. When Sandy found out I was a single mom, she invited John and me over for dinner. She gently pursued the relationship until I felt safe. We are dear friends who still meet together regularly thanks to Sandy's initiative.

Finding common ground is a great place to start. Maybe you're in the choir with someone and you've observed things that draw you to that person. Do you think you could call her up and ask her to coffee one day? For Sandy and me, we needed to take the relationship outside of praise team rehearsal. There is only so much you can learn about a person by talking between songs. Maybe there is a woman in your neighborhood whom you've met a couple of times and she goes out speed walking each morning. Maybe you can invite yourself to be her speed walking partner. I wish relationships just happened, but they don't. They need to be nurtured and developed, and a first step sometimes includes risk.

Logging time together like Faith and I did by walking around several blocks each morning is part of the way relationships develop. Once enough time has been spent together, and as trust grows, we reveal more of ourselves. If we're honest, we can all admit to having some secrets and desperately needing someone to share them with. For you, taking the risk of friendship might mean telling a friend that your teenager is drug addicted or cutting herself and that you're scared. It might mean telling someone about your husband's pornography addiction or your own shopaholic tendencies or issues with food. That's what relationships defined by authenticity look like. We're not perfect; we are works in process, and we need friends to love and support us through the craziness of life.

Deep, healthy friendship—being real and authentic—is also a two-way street. It involves equal disclosure and words of challenge. It requires a willingness to listen for and discern truth, especially when it is spoken by someone who has earned your trust.

A few years after my initial crisis, my son and I had to move out of our neighborhood to a more affordable area. After my move Faith and I couldn't walk around the block anymore, so our connecting took the form of long phone conversations during my commute to the city. One day Faith confronted me on an issue. I had lost fifty pounds, and she was concerned that I might have exchanged my addiction to food for an addiction to spending. In hindsight I am very appreciative of her concern. How did I react in the moment? I said through gritted teeth, "Oh, thank you, Faith, for bringing that to my attention." But once we said goodbye, I hit the "end call" button as hard as I could and screamed out loud in the car, "HOW DARE YOU!"

After a few days and a brief cooling-off period, I called Faith and said, "When you confronted me, weren't you afraid that I might run away from the relationship and not return?"

Faith responded, "Yes, but if I couldn't be honest with you, with whom I have such a solid relationship, who can I be honest with?" That day took us to a deeper level in our friendship.

Many Americans aren't close enough to one other person to call them in case of an emergency, or to come help them if they needed some kind of help. I find that heartbreaking, yet that was me. One day I was reading our online forum that corresponded with our on-air Bible study "A Woman of Moderation," and there was a woman talking about her struggle to lose weight. She realized at age forty-four that she had no friends, no one she could even call to be an accountability partner with her. Are there people in your life you can call in the middle of the night if something goes wrong, if you have an emergency? If not, finding such a friend could be a worthy goal. I know beyond a shadow of a doubt I could call Faith, and there are others: Sandy and Melinda and Nancy and Arloa. And they'd come at 3:00 a.m. if I needed them.

CODEPENDENT RELATIONSHIPS

Not all strong friendships are necessarily healthy. In 2008 and 2009 on *Midday Connection,* we aired a series focused solely on friendships, featuring an on-air Bible study with Dee Brestin centering on her book *The Friendships of Women.* The study prompted me to further evaluate my past friendships. I realized that in the midnineties I developed an unhealthy friendship with a coworker. In hindsight I would call it a codependent relationship.

You can find various definitions of codependency, but basically it is an emotional dependence. There is a stronger and a weaker party, and the weaker controls the stronger. This sounds counterintuitive, but the stronger person takes on the role of a rescuer and is controlled by the neediness in the weaker person. The stronger person will overlook his or her own well-being to care for the needs of the weaker, more dependent individual. Usually both parties fall into some form of what Dee calls relational idolatry.

Angie was a Moody Bible Institute student who worked for me. At the time I was the music director for Moody Radio and producer of a live concert series called the Friday Sing. There were other students working for me also, but Angie was mature, in some ways, beyond her years. Besides working together, Angie and I started performing music together, which tightened our bond. When she graduated from Moody, she was hired full-time to work for me at Moody Radio. We even shared an office. We went from a mentor/mentee relationship to more of a peer friendship. Angie was there for me as I went through my divorce. She was single and had more free time than other friends of mine. She was always available, quick to come to my rescue or help out with babysitting, and she and I had fun hanging out together. I thought maybe I'd found my BFF. I didn't see the signs of codependency at the time. Neither did Angie.

I wasn't the only *Midday Connection* listener who saw myself as a party to a codependent relationship. One listener described a friendship with a Christian friend who had been very supportive during a marital breakup. But eventually the "rescuer" became possessive and jealous. "The demands grew more oppressive to me," she wrote. "The relationship finally ended — painfully — because I just could not be to her what she wanted." Anytime we look to someone else to replace God in our lives, we are in trouble. When emotional dependency takes place, it is the same thing as idolatry.

In her series The Friendships of Women, Dee Brestin told us that when she talks about relational idolatry at conferences or retreats, she usually has a number of women who tell her about friendships that are starting to cross the line into lesbianism. They began as friendship, became overdependent or codependent, and then crossed a line. Not all codependent relationships cross that line; in fact, only a small percentage do, but the bottom line is that in any emotionally dependent relationship, God has been replaced.

Much of this is anchored in our adolescent days. We have to get past the middle school model of BFF, where we have a one-and-only best friend. Another listener emailed that growing up overweight made it hard for her to find good friends, people who wouldn't make fun of her. So in middle school when she found a friend, she entered into a codependent relationship. This listener always wanted to be with her friend and felt bad when her friend wanted to be with others, or when a boyfriend entered the picture. Does that sound familiar? Maybe this has been your struggle too.

God is our only real BFF. We may try to fill that spot with all kinds of things, food, shopping, even other people, but God is the only one who can be that person to us, who can fill that space made only for him. In *My Utmost for His Highest*, Oswald Chambers reflects on the separation of Elijah and Elisha, when Elijah went up to heaven in a chariot of fire.

> It is not wrong for you to depend on your "Elijah" for as long as God gives him to you. But remember that the time will come when he must leave and will no longer be your guide and your leader, because God does not intend for him to stay. Even the thought of that causes you to say, "I cannot continue without my 'Elijah.'" Yet God says you must continue.[1]

Many codependent relationships end painfully. As for my relationship with Angie — we have since talked about our friendship during those years and we are both amazed that God allowed us to preserve it. When one of the parties tries to make changes in the friendship, often the relationship doesn't survive. My friendship with Angie did go on hiatus, but by God's grace we've been able to start fresh, talk about the past, and move forward on a healthy track.

Two things led to this. Angie came to a healthier place where she realized she was giving too much and not receiving anything in return. She started going to counseling for some other issues in her life and the issue of codependency emerged. Angie began to set some healthy boundaries and she started telling me, "No, I can't babysit this week," or "I'm not going to be able to help you with that project; I'll be out with friends then."

I was in counseling at the same time because my marriage was falling apart, and as I moved toward health, I moved further away from Angie. This growing distance was very uncomfortable and bewildering for both of us. We didn't talk about it at the time, but just drifted apart. I'm thankful that we eventually had the courage to address these important issues. We've had the opportunity to see what led us into a kind of relational idolatry, in which both of us were letting the other person take the place of God in our lives.

GOOD FRIENDS LET YOU CRY

Thanks to the friendship and writing of Janet Davis, I came to understand the importance of grief work in my life. I believe some women who struggle with depression could be helped by grieving the losses they've experienced. Please hear me; I'm not saying grieving losses is an answer to depression. I'm saying that I believe most of us don't know how to let go and grieve, and when grieving is left undone, there are consequences that might present themselves, one possibly being depression.

Janet held a retreat for the *Midday Connection* team a few years ago. Her book *The Feminine Soul* had convinced me that grieving losses was important, but I didn't know what this might look like for me. I didn't even know what I needed to grieve. So I asked a direct question. "So, Janet, do I just sit down and start to cry and figure it out as I go?" With a warm smile, she assured me I'd know when the time was right. Issues would present themselves. She also talked a lot about having the space and time to grieve. This got under my skin, because I work full-time. I thought, "When will I have time to grieve?" Like many women,

I've felt that unnerving feeling that if I started to cry I might not be able to stop. So I didn't exactly work at setting the stage to allow myself to grieve. I really was afraid of what might happen.

In the midst of my ongoing dialogue with Janet, I was developing friendships with Nancy Kane and Arloa Sutter, both in professional ministry like me. We had a great deal in common, and I was learning to trust them. We met once a month in my office, and I asked Nancy, who was a college professor as well as a licensed professional in the counseling field, to describe what grieving losses might look like. How would someone know if she was ready to grieve her losses?

Nancy said, "Think of a simmering pot with the contents of the pot bubbling up with steam starting to escape. When you are ready to grieve, the contents of that pot start to ooze out and bubble up, even lifting the lid off the pot." As soon as she finished her explanation, my eyes flooded and the tears began to flow. My pot bubbled over, and I didn't even know what I was crying about.

I'd figured out a long time ago that I wasn't perfect — thanks to a failed marriage and some bungled friendships — but letting my emotions show, or appearing in any way out of control emotionally, was still something I resisted. I'd been comfortable for a number of years saying to friends, "I know I'm a mess." But *showing* it was a different story.

Why are we so afraid of tears? They provide such a soul cleansing and often point us to something important that we need to pay attention to. In his book *Windows of the Soul*, Ken Gire devotes a whole chapter to tears as a window to our souls. In *Whistling in the Dark* Frederick Buechner writes, "Whenever you find tears in your eyes, especially unexpected tears, it is well to pay the closest attention. They are not only telling you something about the secret of who you are, but more often than not

God is speaking to you through them of the mystery of where you have come from and is summoning you to where, if your soul is to be saved, you should go next."[2]

The dam had burst and Arloa grabbed a stack of sticky notes and suggested I list things I was grieving over. "I don't know," I wailed. So she took charge, calling out names or pains she'd heard me mention. She hit the mark any number of times, prompting deep sobs. I remember thinking, "I hope all of my coworkers have gone home." Let's just say I was not a quiet crier.

As Arloa wrote issues and people and circumstances on the sticky notes, I started sensing other things I needed to grieve. She kept writing as I finally took the initiative to call things out. "The loss of my marriage. Coworkers who couldn't handle that I was going through a divorce. The loss of a two-parent home for my son. The loss of a favorite pastor from my past. Sorrow over judging Candy so harshly that day in junior high. The lack of a close family of origin." I thought the crying would never stop. I even called out the loss of my childhood dog, Rosie. I had no idea there was so much that I'd hung on to for so long.

At the beginning of the tears, Arloa said, "Let's get down on the floor, and we'll weep with you." All three of us sat on the floor. It reminded me of Old Testament stories where people sat in sackcloth and ashes on the ground and grieved together. My friends had brought their sackcloth and come to sit with me in the ashes of my grief. That's what friends do. Please remember this, if you remember nothing else from this chapter. Friends cry in front of other friends. If we can't be real with those we are closest to, we will live a lonely existence.

PRAYING FOR A FRIEND

That day in my office I understood a new level of friendship. How did I get there? By opening up little by little and not being afraid of looking like the mess that I am. Do you think you could take some of those same baby steps? The first might be asking God to send you a friend.

Mindy Caliguire tells the story that a neighbor of hers prayed for over a year for God to bring a friend into her life. That friend was Mindy, who moved in across the street. I usually get tired of praying for something after two weeks. Can we persevere in prayer for a friendship?

A listener wrote in admitting that it was hard to wait for God to send her a friend. She continued, "Our cleaning lady at work is becoming a very dear friend. Who knew? Others may pass her by as she carries a mop and broom, but I'm finding a wonderful prayer partner in her!"

"Who knew?"—exactly! She's been waiting for a friend when God has already sent her a good candidate.

I would urge you to trust God, to believe God will provide that person or persons, and begin praying today. God met me in my need on the floor of my office with two friends willing to weep with me. I've had many failed attempts at friendship, but God brought along the right women at just the right time. He can do the same for you.

DISCUSSION QUESTIONS

1. Reflect on your past and present friendships. What has been the most difficult part for you in developing friendships?

2. In what ways do small groups help the process of developing friendships?

3. What can make friendships with women seemingly more difficult than male friendships?

4. Describe a time when a friend betrayed you. Have you come

to a place of forgiveness so you can move forward into other friendships? Could you help someone else get to that point?

5. What is one step you can take toward beginning a friendship with someone?

6. Friendships take time and need nurturing. What things are needed to nurture a friendship?

7. Take some time to do a short study on some of the great friendships in Scripture. What were some of the characteristics of the relationship between Ruth and Naomi, or David and Jonathan? Dee Brestin's *The Friendships of Women* Bible study (Cook, 2006) can help you dig deeper into this topic.

chapter three

DREAMING — AND WEEPING — FOR OUR CHILDREN

What Women Tell Me:
I often feel if my children are misbehaving then I must be doing something wrong. They are either modeling my mistakes or I am lacking in some way as a mother. I constantly am fighting against my perfectionist tendencies.

•••

WILLIAM WORDSWORTH WROTE, "THE CHILD IS father of the Man." Taking some poetic license, maybe we could feminize the phrase: "The Child is mother of the Woman." Our childhoods influence our life stories — or at least that was true in my case.

In my parents' generation life just "happened" to women. Certainly that was the case for my mom. In rural northern

Maine, she attended a one-room schoolhouse where she skipped several grades. At fifteen she graduated from high school and left home to attend a conservative Christian college. There she met the "man of her dreams," my dad. At age sixteen — yes, sixteen — she got married. At eighteen she had my twin brothers. At age twenty-two, she had me. You know that thing called childhood? She didn't have one. It's no surprise that my parents didn't give me much life direction. It wasn't something that their parents had given to them.

My mother sent me off to boarding school with a dream — that I would love and serve the Lord. That I would get to know him and his Word, and that I would be happy. I'm not sure in which order those desires came. I believe there has been a lot of sadness in my mother's life, even though outwardly everything looks good. She has a beautiful family that at first glance looks nice and spit-polished. But she gained it at the expense of her own childhood.

My grandfather was a farmer and wanted a boy but instead got my mom. Imagine not being wanted for who you are. She did all she could to live up to his expectations. As an only child she could work circles around the hired help on the family farm.

As I headed off to boarding school, she wanted me to have the happiness that eluded her. My parents drove me south from our home in Plymouth Meeting, Pennsylvania. When we arrived in Toccoa Falls, Georgia, it had the feel of any town in the Deep South in August. Hot, humid, and everyone a bit too polite for my liking. A syrupy sweetness accompanied every conversation. When I met my roommate from southern Illinois, I was elated. There was nothing sugary about Bebe. She was authentic to the core, although a bit tactless.

After my dorm room was set up, the goodbyes began. We did it with a mixture of emotions, but neither my mom nor I expressed our true feelings. We pasted on the expected smile that belied what was underneath, and then my mom and dad headed north. I went back into my dorm room carrying some of the same dreams my mom had for me.

Though I didn't see the pattern at the time, when I left home at age fifteen to attend Christian boarding high school, I followed the pattern my mother had set years earlier. A fifteen-year-old has little self-awareness. I received a quality education at first Toccoa Falls and then Ben Lippen School. But I didn't learn much about myself.

I knew theologically that I was a sinner saved by grace; Jesus had died for *my* sins. But I can't say I felt like a sinner. Oh, maybe an occasional flash of envy for a classmate, but I took some pride in my holy rigor — daily devotions and so on. Who was I? A good and fervent Christian girl blossoming into womanhood. On any deeper level I didn't even know what questions to ask. I had little training — formally taught or informally modeled — on how to know myself. So the same thing that was true of my mom was repeated one generation later with me. She had a truncated childhood; so did I.

At age fifteen, like my mother, I gave the impression of being confident and self-assured. Because of how I presented myself, my teachers, dorm parents, and mission leaders all assumed I had some insight into and ability to discern what I was good at, what I was temperamentally suited for, what direction I wanted to take, what purpose I wanted to pursue. Unfortunately, presentation is only half the picture.

I did have an interest in psychology, but the most affordable college didn't offer that as a major, so I set that interest aside. Not long ago my mother told me how surprised she was that I didn't major in psychology in college. Imagine my shock, in my midforties, to hear that I might have been able to pursue that major. At the time I was not encouraged to do so even by those who were close to me and in the best position to provide counsel, and I assumed those college options were too expensive, so I dropped the idea.

Let me back up. Maybe I overstated what the adults around me assumed I could figure out about my life journey. Mostly they assumed that a man would come along and rescue me. His vision would become our vision. We'd make children—perfect children, maybe three, a pair and a spare—and people would rise up and call me blessed. In the meantime I should go to college.

As I prepared to head off to Moody Bible Institute, the options for a Christian woman seemed minimal. This was a Bible school that specialized in training for ministry, not secular professions. I eventually graduated with a major in Bible/theology. Maybe I just wasn't paying attention, but at Bible college I learned a lot more about sin—the very specific list of don'ts—than about the realities of grace.

MY FIRST SIGNIFICANT FAILURE

By April of my senior year, a rescuer of the male variety was nowhere in sight, so I auditioned to tour with the Internationals starting a month after graduation. My year with the singing group concluded. To regroup, I went back home—my parents now lived in Kansas City, Kansas—still without a plan. In hindsight I am most thankful for the doctrine of God's sovereignty. At least Someone had a plan!

For a while I worked as a music specialist for a small Christian publishing company that owned two retail stores. But frankly I felt bored. Looking for a way to invest myself, I saw a great need for a youth director in my urban church. The line for the position wasn't exactly long. I had a theological degree from a Bible college. I got the job. I figured, how hard can it be to rally some kids together and talk about Jesus?

But nothing in my youthful experience or college training prepared me for what was about to happen. Maybe it was a little like parenthood: I had no idea what to expect or what I was doing.

I didn't have the benefit of being a youth ministries major, but I had plenty of passion and I knew I needed to love on those kids. I knew they had no template for Christian living, and most had no relationship with Jesus. They came to youth group because their parents made them, or there was nothing better to do on a Sunday night.

I was excited to dig in to my newfound assignment. I tried to make our times together fun. And they were. Working at a Christian bookstore, I bought every Youth Specialties book I could get my hands on. Mike Yaconelli and Wayne Rice were crazy guys. I had no original thought when it came to fun for the group. It all came from Yac and Rice. We'd play goofy relay races with oranges and chewing gum, games like pie tin toss, anything to capture attention and build community. My measure of success was that the youth group ran smoothly, the kids kept coming back, and I got to teach from Scripture each Sunday night, even though that was the shortest part of the evening.

We met each Sunday morning for a Sunday school class, then each Sunday night in the church annex, a small home across the street from the main church building. We sat in a circle. On a good night there were eight to ten of us. I started with some basics about faith with plenty of opportunities to present the gospel. I prayed that the application part — living pure lives, resisting sin — of the teaching was sinking in.

I had dreams for these kids, but as I looked at who attended, my dreams weren't realistic. I pictured them, by my sheer example alone, deciding to attend Moody Bible Institute or some other reputable Bible college. As hard as I tried, they had no real desire for spiritual things.

I remember one Sunday night asking them to bring their favorite music. The stack of music ranged from Black Sabbath to Def Leppard to Motley Crue to Judas Priest. I obviously didn't know what I was getting into. After they told me their favorite song, I asked them to read the lyrics to the group. When the lyrics became R-rated, they quit reading and determined, at least to my face, to rid their collections of those particularly bad albums. Looking back, I did a good job shaming, not such a good job teaching and training. But they continued to come back. I guess you can't underestimate the effect of someone showing interest and showing up, even if they are doing a marginal job.

Most of these teens had no encouragement at home. Many came from families with no history of college attendance, not even solid job histories. Poverty was a reality for most. Ambition was virtually nonexistent. Who was I to think I could make a difference? I certainly knew nothing would happen apart from a work of God, but I wasn't quite sure God could make a difference either.

In theory, I was at a good place to lead kids to Christ and deeper into relationship with him. I was well schooled in Scripture, and I was at a good place to help move teens closer to Christ as long as there were no glitches in the program. The problem was, I was working with people, teenage people, and glitches come with the territory.

I might have fared better, but for most of my life I'd seen knee-jerk reactions to sin. I hadn't been adequately taught "how" to think, only "what" to think, and so the message I heard during my Bible college years focused on the fact that everything was black and white. Easy answers were plentiful, and as a Bible college graduate, I thought I *did* have all the answers.

But after almost a year, when all, and I mean *all*, of the teenage girls in the youth group became pregnant, my Bible college answers just disintegrated. I remember Megan missing youth group for two weeks in a row. I asked Jeanette if Megan was sick and the group started to snicker. It was all I could do to hold it together when Jeanette said, "If by sick you mean morning sickness, then yeah, she's sick." Where do you go with that? What do you say to the group then? I said, "Oh." That was all I could muster; then I moved on. I didn't even have the wherewithal to call Megan and ask how she was doing and what happened. Honestly, I didn't know if I had built up enough in her emotional bank account to ask those kinds of questions, so I did nothing, hoping she would come back to youth group soon, and she did.

I don't even remember when I found out about Ruby. Next was Jeanette, who snickered at Megan until it was her turn. News about the rest is all a blur. Whether they just wanted someone to love, or someone who would love them, I don't know. In most of the girls' families, unwed pregnancy was a pattern of generational sin. What I *am* sure of is I didn't have a clue what to do.

Some of the families were more plugged in to the life of the church than others, so a baby shower was arranged for those kids. I didn't know if a baby shower was appropriate or not. How do you discourage the sin but love the sinner? I didn't know. With mixed emotions, which I couldn't even sort out, I attended Ruby's baby shower. All I could muster during the event was a polite smile. I'm sure I kept looking at my watch. I couldn't wait to escape back to the parsonage next door. I was glad I had a full-time job as a diversion, because the part-time one wasn't going so well.

Before the youth group could become a nursery, I received a call from Chicago. Someone at Moody had recommended me for a job at Moody Radio. I was excited about this new job prospect, but I left the Kansas City church feeling defeated — and relieved that I could blast out of town permanently. I was in way over my head. I didn't know what to do with or about the girls.

As I reflect on those days, I realize that my first impulse wasn't to try to do something to help them fall deeply in love with Jesus. I just wanted them to stop their bad behavior.

I knew that I needed to show love and not condemnation, but every bone in my body wanted to jump up and down and point out the sin. I didn't want to shame the girls in my youth group, but I wanted desperately to do something to make them stop sinning. Or maybe I just wanted the visual reminder of their sin to go away so I wasn't confronted with it week in and week out, confronted with my own sense of failure and shame because I felt their failures reflected on me. Great leader, huh? I had such dreams for them. What had I done wrong? It was in some ways my first crisis of faith — and in a role that seemed almost parental.

A MOTHER'S PAIN

I sense that some version of those very questions haunt Christian mothers across the country. What have I done wrong? Where is God? How can I live with the shame? What do I do now? The questions arise particularly when our children sin in an obvious, evident way. Teen pregnancy is on that list of hard-to-hide issues.

I can't tell you how many moms, when we've covered the topic of teen mothers on *Midday Connection*, have emailed saying how alone they felt when this happened to their daughters.

"The world fell apart when she told me." Or how a church member had quietly suggested abortion or disentanglement. "We were encouraged by Christian 'family' to 'shun' her." Or how fingers had been pointed because they obviously hadn't done a good job of training their daughter.

One woman writes, "How can we let our teens know that they should abstain, but that if they do get pregnant they should come home and tell their parents? I can't help but believe that teens may abort because they can't face their family and friends."

Whole chapters of other books can address the importance of abstinence and/or the prevention of teen pregnancy. But laying out parental guidelines isn't my purpose here. Here I'd like to discuss the way we handle crises in our lives, view our parental failures, and engender trust with our children.

OUR JOURNEY OF FAITH

I read emails from hurting women that often show that they desperately want someone to tell them exactly what to do. Isn't that what we all want, especially in times of crisis? How often have you said, "I wish God would just write it in the sky, or hit me with a lightning bolt"? The older I get, or maybe more importantly, the deeper I get in my relationship with Christ and the more I know God's Word, the more I understand that it's about the journey of faith, not the knee-jerk reactions we have in a moment of crisis. It's about how we ride the waves, not run from them or control them.

Let me go back to my story. I wondered why God allowed me to have the experience of directing that Kansas City youth group where all the girls became pregnant on my watch. Why did I have to experience the discomfort of not knowing what to do about it, of feeling like my faith was failing me? Hindsight being 20/20, I see how I thought it was all up to me. This is usually how black-and-white thinking plays out. I had all the answers; therefore I was the one responsible for everyone's behavior. As a budding Pharisee, I was the righteous one trying to keep everyone else on track. It breaks my heart now to see how unwilling or unable I was to fully surrender to God and let him do the work that only he can do.

I now see where God has brought me. He knew that my black-and-white Christianity of the early 1980s wouldn't stand the test of time, so he led me on a journey of learning how to live with the questions, to live with the tensions that our life of faith creates. This would be the first, not the last, experience of brokenness. And my first, not my last, sense of being a failure in regard to leading the young.

OUR FAILURES IN PERSPECTIVE

In my late twenties I did marry, though maybe for all the wrong reasons. On a June day I stood in a church and made promises I wanted to keep. My father walked me down the aisle and my mother sat stoically in the front row. She didn't romanticize marriage; in fact, she often told me, "It's not all that glamorous, Anita. There is the laundry to do, the dishes to wash, the meals to get ready. But you've got someone to take care of you." I think she hoped she wouldn't have to take care of me her whole life, that maybe I'd find some financial security beyond what she and my dad could provide. I think financial security might have been the biggest dream she had for me.

Eventually things fell apart, but from that union I was blessed with a son. John is a bright light in my life today, but the early years of mothering him tell a different story. Some women are made for babies; some aren't. I barely survived the baby years. I struggled with postpartum depression for two years, which certainly didn't help. John had a couple of minor complications at birth. Nothing life threatening, but enough to keep the two of us from bonding.

Breast-feeding was another challenge. I tried and tried to breast-feed, burning up a hotline to a lactation consultant, but it didn't do any good. John was losing weight, and the doctor determined that I needed to use a bottle. I felt like a total failure as a mother. I don't know how you can feel guilty over something you have no control over, but I did. I suppose those well-meaning mothers who kept telling me the "one more thing" I should have tried before giving up helped the guilt train keep running down the tracks.

I remember when John was almost twelve years old and needed a new pair of tennis shoes. Usually I headed to Walmart or Kmart, but I waited a little too long to do my back-to-school shopping and the inventory was depleted, so we headed to a higher-end shoe store. When we got there I noticed there weren't any tennis shoes with Velcro straps available in John's size. The shoe store salesgirl said, "Of course there aren't; he's too big for that. Do you mean to tell me he doesn't know how to tie his own shoes?" Okay, just back up the guilt dump truck and open the tailgate. I felt shame, guilt, and anything else negative I could pile on myself. She was right. I'd never taught John to tie his shoes. She did it in about five minutes; then we bought a pair of tie shoes and away we went.

Just as nothing in my youthful experience had prepared me for being a youth director, nothing had prepared me for the overwhelming nature of parenthood. My greatest fear in parenthood had been that I'd be tired all the time — and I was. Depressed and tired and not quite sure how to relate to this bundle of need. In time, through God's grace, I made a lot of positive changes. My son was growing to maturity. I could see that I was passing along to him the best of my family heritage. And I lived in faith that my dreams for him—though nonspecific—would come true: I wanted him to be a godly Christian.

ENGENDERING TRUST IN OUR CHILDREN

Mothers often ask how they can maintain standards for their children—teach them right from wrong—and yet expect that their children will be honest with them when they get in trouble or disobey. It's a hard question and the dynamics of every family are different. But I was deeply struck recently when I read a personal essay titled "Facing the Truth" by Caroline Langston, a mother of two young children. Caroline describes a recent morning when she just couldn't seem to motivate her young son Alex to quit his dawdling and get himself out the door to school. Outwardly she kept her cool, but inwardly she grew so frustrated that, when no one was looking, she stomped on a favorite toy of his, a cheap small airplane. She placed it in a wastebasket and thought no more of it.

A few days later her son happened upon the crushed plane in the wastebasket. To get him to stop crying, she told him she'd broken it by accident. But the lie niggled. She realized it had been a sorry attempt to cover herself, like Adam and Eve in Eden. Before the end of the day, she went and found Alex to confess her wrongdoing. It wasn't an accident, she said. She admitted she'd felt angry and hurtful. In word and demeanor she said she was sorry. And how did Alex respond? He stared at her a minute and finally said, "Mama, you shouldn't have done that.... I'm still mad, but I forgive you."[1]

I myself remember the day that I stood by John's bed and said, "John, I was so impatient when you were little. Remember when I'd tell you near bedtime that Mom isn't a good mom after 8:30 p.m.? I struggled, really struggled at being a mom. I wished those days away, and frankly felt I didn't do a very good job as a parent."

Now maybe my confession was a bit too vulnerable or weighty for a then freshman in high school. John's response melted my heart much like Alex's response to Caroline melted hers. He said, "Mom, I kind of knew you were struggling. I knew you did the best you could, and look at me — I turned out all right, didn't I?"

"Yes, John, you did. God is so good to take what we've got and make it into something more than we ever could."

Many parents hold to the belief that they should be stoic and hard-line and never admit wrong. If we are honest with our children about our shortcomings, we open the door for them to be honest with us. John is now a senior in high school, and I'm grateful I learned to admit when I was wrong and ask for forgiveness. There will always be tensions in parenting, but if we can live in those tensions in an honest way, we pave the way for our children to grow into healthy adults.

A MOTHER'S DREAM

God finally taught me that I couldn't do a very good job with any of the kids in my Kansas City youth group or any other hurting person who crossed my path until I saw that I was broken, until I saw my own sin. Until I saw the measure of his grace for me, I couldn't adequately communicate his grace to anyone else. Henri Nouwen said we are all wounded healers, and what a relief that is! The full extent of that lesson was years in the making for me, but God in his grace didn't give up on me.

And I will not give up on my efforts to bring up my child — my son, John — in the way of the Lord.

My mother's dream for me was that I would be a woman blessed by God. I'm not sure I'm who or where she expected me to be, but I think she would smile to read this verse, hidden away in Psalm 144:12: "May our sons in their youth be like plants full grown, our daughters like corner pillars cut for the structure of a palace" (ESV).

It's the dream I have for my son—and for you and your children, whether they're maturing according to your plan or struggling to find their way.

DISCUSSION QUESTIONS

1. If you are a mother, what were your early hopes and dreams regarding motherhood?

2. What were or are your greatest challenges as a mother?

3. Have you ever felt that you've messed up as a parent? How have you dealt with those feelings?

4. How can you engender trust and authenticity with your children?

5. If your child or someone else's child has failed in some public way, how can you best support them without condoning their behavior?

chapter four

YOU'D BETTER WATCH OUT

What Women Tell Me:
I pleaded with the pastors and elders to come alongside my husband. I bared my soul and exposed the deep pain regarding his abuse. I was told that my heart was wicked.

•••

I CAN STILL REMEMBER THE PROGRAM, even the year: 1998. I was sitting in the producer's chair for *Midday Connection*. Andrea Fabry was the host. She'd already introduced Paul Hegstrom, the day's guest. The phone lines lit up. Every line was full with incoming calls. The phone answerer took down caller information as fast as she could. I took a few incoming calls to help out before the real job of producing began.

When you answer the *Midday* phone line, you ask the caller's name, city, and state and the call letters of the radio station she hears the program on, and then you take down her question or comment before getting her phone number — to call her back if her question makes it on the air.

As producer, I read through the call slips that were in a pile in front of me. The producer needs to listen to the direction of the program and decide which question makes the most sense to put on the air first. I called to prep the first caller we wanted to put on the air. "Hello, this is *Midday Connection*. We've picked your question to be put on the air. You'll need to turn your radio off or all the way down so there won't be any feedback. I'm going to put you on hold. You'll hear the program through your phone, and when the host welcomes you and says your name, you're on the air. Go ahead and briefly state your question or comment." Usually the caller just says okay. This first caller said, "I want to remain anonymous."

Usually the guest and host talk for about ten minutes before the producer puts the first call on. This particular day calls were coming in so fast I put a call up on the screen right away. The producer and host can talk to each other via a computer screen during the program. Once the caller is on hold, the producer types the first name of the caller, her city and state, and a brief synopsis of the question or comment so the host has an idea of what the caller will say. That way if the caller gets way off track, the host can guide her back to the original question. You'd be surprised what happens when nerves kick in.

As I started to line up the calls, I noticed the pattern. Every caller wanted to remain anonymous. No surprise, I guess, considering the topic. It was the first time *Midday Connection* addressed domestic violence. It was also a day that would change my life. Even as I prepped callers to be on the air, I strained to hear everything Paul Hegstrom and Andrea were saying. Paul's discussion and definitions were broader than physical violence.

He outlined patterns of emotional, psychological, and verbal abuse that all qualify under the term "domestic violence." *Walking on eggshells. Living in fear. Never knowing what might set someone off.* It was like the Santa Claus song turned on its tail: *You'd better watch out.*

When the show finally ended and Andrea had thanked Paul and said goodbye, I walked briskly into the studio to talk with her. My heart was racing; I wanted to run into the studio, but I didn't want anyone to think there was a problem. I still can't believe I blurted it out. I said, "That's my life. He's describing my life. He's been like a fly on the wall in my house. I didn't know it wasn't okay."

Andrea just stared at me for a moment; then she started asking me some leading questions. In that brief conversation I knew I needed help. I called and made an appointment with a counselor.

Back in the late 1990s we sold cassettes of *Midday Connection*. A good day meant selling fifty copies of the broadcast. We sold hundreds of copies that day. Then we did something we had never done before. We asked the guest if he would be available to come back on the program the next day. When he said yes, we called and rescheduled the originally scheduled guest. Both Andrea and I felt prompted by God to make the change. Once again every caller wanted to remain anonymous, and we sold hundreds of copies of the program. I remember thinking, "Why have I never heard this talked about in the church before, in my church?"

Here's the scenario laid out by one listener—the daughter of a deacon—who called herself Anonymous. When she was a child, what people perceived as her "perfect little family" showed up at church every Sunday. But no one there realized the horrors of their Sunday afternoons. If a man at coffee hour had been so bold as to shake his wife's hand or smile at her, Deacon Dad accused his wife of "horrible things." Anonymous wrote, "I can remember the beatings as if they were yesterday." When her mom risked talking to someone at the church, the deacon was confronted. The result? He denied the abuse and went home and punished his wife. In time, this wife and mother turned to friends outside the church and "had the courage and strength to get out of the situation." The daughter's email ends: "I wish the church had been what it should have been for her."

The frequency with which we address domestic violence on *Midday Connection* has increased; since the program is geared toward women, you might expect our awareness to be heightened. One of the questions that began gnawing at me after my own eyes were opened to this topic was, "Does God see women? Does he hurt when women are wronged and abused?"

DOES GOD SEE WOMEN IN DISTRESS?

Certainly if ever there was a woman who seemed invisible, it was Hagar. In Genesis 16 we enter the part of Hagar's story where she has been mistreated by Sarai and runs away into the desert. There she is confronted by an angel who asks her, "Where have you come from, and where are you going?"

"I'm running away," she answers. Hagar is running from her abusive and jealous mistress. Sarai greatly mistreated her maidservant even though Hagar performed her duty of bearing a child by Abraham when Sarai couldn't. Even though this was one of Hagar's purposes in the household, Sarai couldn't handle it once it happened. Hagar showed up Sarai's deficiencies, and her very presence was an offense to Sarai.

For now the angel tells Hagar to return home. That's not what Hagar wanted to hear, and frankly not what I wanted to hear in this story either. But God doesn't send us on suicide missions. He is with us and he had redemptive purposes in mind here. Up to this point in the story, neither Abraham nor Sarai calls Hagar by name, but the angel calls her by name. The angel tells her that she will bear a son and "shall name him Ishmael [which means 'God hears'], for the Lord has heard of your misery" (Genesis 16:11).

What did Hagar say in return? "You are the God who sees me" (Genesis 16:13). Carolyn Custis James in her book *Lost Women of the Bible* says of Hagar, "She gives God a name. No one else in Scripture—male or female—ever names God. Hagar does. She names him El Roi: 'the God who sees me.' The new name she gives to God expresses her most basic theological conviction: she is not invisible to God."[1]

DO I SEE WOMEN IN DISTRESS?

Several years ago I went on a trip to Israel with Moody Bible Institute. My new husband, Mike, and I had the privilege of going along with 650 of our closest friends. It was the most well-run, well-organized tour I've ever been a part of. I was struck with awe as I literally walked where Jesus walked on the southern steps of the temple in Jerusalem. Taking an old fishing boat out on the Sea of Galilee made the Gospel passages come alive. Standing on top of Mount Arbel, able to see where Jesus spent most of his ministry days, helped me realize the geography was no bigger than my town and a few surrounding suburbs connected together. But I was struck by more than the geography and ancient history of Israel.

One day we toured the Yad Vashem Holocaust Museum in Jerusalem. As we walked from gallery to gallery, I viewed horrific photographs and videos. They should have made me sick, but they didn't. I felt relatively little emotion, so I opened an ongoing dialogue (or maybe it was a monologue) with God.

"Lord, why isn't this getting to me?" I'd walk to the next exhibit: "Lord, this doesn't seem to be affecting me. Why?"

Then I turned a corner and there it was: a large picture of women, only women, all with their heads shaved. Hollow eyes. Gaunt, sunken-in cheeks. They wore matching striped prison-camp garb. At this sight, I fell apart. I lost it, or as much as I could in the midst of the sea of people streaming through the museum. Tears ran down my cheeks. I stood there taking in the faces of the women. That picture — of women oppressed, of women in bondage — wrecked me. It expanded my awareness of something I already knew in the depths of my soul. God was calling me to take a more active role in raising awareness — awareness that disrespect toward, mistreatment of, and violence against women are wrong.

MY JOURNEY

I grew up with a low view of women. I didn't think women were important or had things of value to say. They weren't, in my estimation, involved in important things. This view was not overtly modeled in my family of origin, but it was there as well as everywhere else I looked, including the church.

My early memories are of life in northern Maine. On the farm you had value if you were working hard out in the field. As I mentioned before, my mother was an only child and needed to be the boy my grandfather wanted. She worked just as hard as any man on the farm and was valued more highly if she could keep up with them. In the little country church my grandparents and mother attended, all the deacons were men, and of course the pastor was a man. All the Sunday school teachers were women, but back then it wasn't seen as a valuable job. Everyone assumed it was beneath men to teach children.

When I went to boarding high school and Christian college,

women couldn't run for student council president. The highest post they could attain was vice president, and some guys thought it was a stretch for a woman to hold that post. Cooking and cleaning, the household domestic duties, though necessary, weren't deemed important either. My mother reinforced that thinking prior to my getting married when she said, "It's a lot of hard work, Anita. There's the cooking, the dishes, the cleaning." She made me think I was signing up for years of hard labor. Come to think of it . . .

Even though many things have changed, I've not yet seen a woman as president of the United States. Many still argue a woman cannot do the job. The point is, in my growing-up years I didn't see many women develop their gifts or act in any leadership capacity in society or the church. Society has changed—the church, not so quickly.

I thought I'd moved beyond some of my low views of women. A couple of years ago a listener sent me a book titled *The Feminine Soul* that made me see otherwise. There was something about this book, maybe just the title, that grabbed me. Certainly no one had ever talked to me about my feminine soul! As I started reading, I became very emotional at these words penned by author Janet Davis:

> Have you ever heard a sermon addressing or even acknowledging that men and women differ spiritually? Have you ever seen different growth paradigms put forth for the different sexes? Has anyone in your church ever talked about how men and women sin differently? If they have, you attend a very unusual church. Most of us assume that spirituality is unisex.[2]

I sure had assumed that spirituality was unisex. I read these words in March 2007, as a forty-seven-year-old Christian woman, and it was the first time this thought had been introduced to me. I have to admit, it took me a few months to get over my anger that none of the male teachers I'd listened to over the course of my lifetime had ever suggested this.

The Feminine Soul brought to the forefront a lifetime of feeling inferior in the church because I was a woman. Feeling like I didn't matter, feeling that I couldn't contribute solely because of my gender. I know this thought doesn't pervade the entire church, but it was the predominant message I received in the stream of evangelicalism in which I grew up. I realized an injustice had been committed.

I have a long history with people, both friends and relatives, who have a strong sense of justice. I didn't think I was one of them. I just thought I was attracted to those with a strong sense of justice. But then I noticed it might actually be in my genes. I first identified this family trait as I read Dan Allender's book *To Be Told: Know Your Story, Shape Your Future* and its intense and demanding (highly recommended) workbook/study guide. I interviewed Dan, but what sold me on reading the whole book and doing the workbook was what I read on the back cover: "Everyone wants clearer guidance from God on what to do with their future … as people listen to the stories of their lives, they identify the themes that God has written there. They begin to understand both the hope and the heartache, and they receive specific guidance for the future that fits who they are." I knew I wanted that and didn't yet have it!

As I started looking at my history, especially on my mom's side, I saw a generational pattern of concern for people who lived out, as best they knew how, a belief in "justice for all." My grandfather, a farmer in northern Maine, always hired Native Americans to work on the farm, when his other farming buddies wouldn't. Prejudice was only part of the reason other farmers wouldn't hire them. It was more work to employ those from the Micmac and Maliseet tribes. My mom told me stories of how she, as a young teen, would drive the car into town to pick them up. They didn't have their own transportation. She'd pound on the doors of the shacks the workers lived in, waking them up, and then waiting while they dressed for work.

My grandpa also hired more than one mentally challenged individual from the community. When I was nine or ten and old enough to pick raspberries, I picked alongside Becky one day. She didn't always make sense, but she told me about her family, including two sons who also picked berries and other vegetables. She looked a bit odd with her crooked mouth, missing teeth, and ragged, mismatched clothes.

My grandfather always treated his workers with dignity and fairness. He was a well-loved man, evidenced by his standing-room-only funeral. I remember going with him on a weekend afternoon to visit the town alcoholic. My grandfather looked in on him to make sure he was okay; he would give him some handyman business and talk with him about Jesus. I saw his great example of biblical compassion and care for the poor and disenfranchised.

My mom carried on that legacy. As a pastor's wife, she answered many knocks at the door. In an urban setting, where she and my dad lived later in their ministry, those knocks often meant someone was in need. When I was away at college in the 1980s, my mom told me stories about groups of Hispanic men riding the trains north and jumping off in Kansas City to go find food. Their church was not far from the railroad yard, and men would knock on my parents' door hoping it was the pastor's home, because it was next to the church. Mom would usually send the group to the picnic table in the backyard. She'd gather all the bread she had in the house along with jars of peanut butter and jelly. Then she would make a big pitcher of iced tea, hand them some knives to spread the PB&J, and let them have at it. I've heard her say countless times, "I would never see anyone go hungry."

At home for Christmas break one year, I remember three different times when I heard a late-night knock on the door. My parents were used to it, but it was a little frightening to me. Each time it was a homeless person looking for a place to spend the night. Kansas City had a very active city mission just a few miles from the church. My dad would ask questions to ascertain the need. If he deemed it necessary to give money, he relied on the church's benevolence fund. Often Dad would drive the person down to the mission to get clean clothes, a shower, and a good night's sleep.

It's no surprise that I'm now married to a man who works with an inner-city ministry that includes an outreach to the homeless.

How has this concern for justice found its way into the reality of my life? As a middle schooler I was not afraid to stick up for the underdog, making a place at the lunchroom table for the girl who was alone, creating a community for the misfits. After all, I was one of them.

Later, as a working woman, I got called into my boss's office after I wrote a letter to the editor, reacting to an article in the college-student newspaper about campus childcare. I wasn't a student, but the paper was delivered to students, faculty, and staff alike. The article touched my justice nerve, and I couldn't sit by and say nothing. I'm sure the fact that I was seven months pregnant at the time and looking into my own childcare options had nothing to do with it! I disagreed with two major points: that most employees were primary wage earners, and that there weren't many working mothers who would benefit from onsite childcare. I believed the administration was closing its eyes to the realities of the workforce, and hence my letter to the editor. It was the first time I acted on my desire for justice, especially for women.

But not my last. When my church moved from traditional to contemporary worship, I took a more active role in leading music. I had been doing so for more than a year when my role was questioned because of my gender. I did some research and talked further with the music director. I confess I was going to quit being part of the music ministry completely if the decision fell against me. Not because of sour grapes, but because I believed a statement needed to be made. All too often in church, decisions are made that hurt people and are unbiblical. I decided others needed to know. I didn't have to go that far. I was allowed to continue leading worship when it was deemed that I was acting under the authority of the minister of music. It was a bittersweet decision for me. I was stirred up and continued to read and study about women's roles in the church.

Because of my visible role with the letter to the editor and the worship leading controversy, I had several women come to me privately who had experienced injustice and were living in significant pain. One situation had to do with a sexually addicted spouse; the other had to do with sexual harassment in the workplace. God continued to bring injustice into my path. I never went looking for it.

I now see that the theme of my life is to communicate freedom to women. That theme manifests itself in a variety of ways, from helping women experience the freedom of the gospel in their life, to finding freedom from a debilitating addiction, to walking toward freedom from domestic violence.

In Christian institutions I've seen great injustices perpetrated on women. I trust I've learned when to speak up and when to hold my tongue, when to be gracious and when to be testy. I've sought the Lord on many occasions to see what he would have me do. Almost always the right thing has been to do something. More often the question is what to do, how to do it, and what attitude to have while carrying out the action. Jesus stood up for the oppressed; how can we do any less?

PURPOSE AND HOLY DISCONTENT

Time and again, I've thanked God for bringing me around the corner to that picture in the Yad Vashem museum that day. He helped confirm his purpose for my life.

Purpose can be a tricky thing. Sometimes when God calls us to something difficult, or something that has a draining dynamic to it, we can start to pull away, struggling to stay with it for the long haul. At a Willow Creek Arts Conference, Bill Hybels mentioned the concept of "holy discontent." When God puts something on or in your heart and you feel like pulling back and walking away, you can't. In my background it might have been called a conviction—a strong inner sense that God wants you to pray about or act on something. Hybels suggested something that is completely counterintuitive: we need to *feed* that sense of holy discontent.

I did this unknowingly on a vacation several years ago, when I selected some reading material to take along—two solid and helpful Christian books, Dan Allender's *To Be Told* and Ken Gire's *Windows of the Soul*. I also thought I should have a novel, something lighter to read. So I bought *A Thousand Splendid Suns*. I didn't know what it was about, but it had received great reviews as a *New York Times* bestseller. Those who know the content are already laughing at my choice of a "light" novel.

A Thousand Splendid Suns recounts the daily lives of Afghani women who are forced to wear the comprehensively covering

Burqa garments — from the top of the head to the ground — when they step out of the house or appear in front of any man other than their husband. Because I live in a Chicago suburb that has one of the largest mosques in all of Chicagoland, I had seen hijabs before, the traditional Muslim head covering for women. I have also seen women wearing burqas, though not in my suburb. But I had not heard a burqa described.

As portrayed in *A Thousand Splendid Suns,* burqas are incredibly heavy. Women wearing them often bear more than physical weight: they also endure an emotional weight. Burqas can be stifling when the weather is warm. And with a burqa, your face is completely covered except for your eyes. A burqa completely blocks your peripheral vision. You look out either through a tiny slit in the fabric or more often through a small mesh screen. The most disheartening thing I learned about a burqa is that it allows bruises and knocked-out teeth to go unseen. A husband can abuse his wife in any number of ways, and no one knows. Just to be clear, not every woman wearing a burqa is hiding bruises, but that possibility exists because of the complete body coverage.

I did not realize how this novel would affect me. It was like walking around the corner in the Yad Vashem museum all over again. But I needed that dose of being up close and personal with what God had called me to. I didn't realize I had stepped away from "communicating freedom to women." Do you know what kind of program I booked on *Midday Connection* as soon as I returned from that vacation? You guessed it! A program on domestic violence. Those hours spent reading did more than just engage my mind about Afghanistan and Muslim women. My heart and mind were turned again toward God's call on my life: to communicate freedom to women.

PATTERNS OF ABUSE

Through the years we've had some great guests on *Midday Connection* talking about domestic violence. Some of the things women have told me have broken my heart.

Another Anonymous, a mother of three, admitted she'd never imagined she would find herself putting up with abuse. But she did so because she so desperately wanted to keep her family intact. Ultimately she filed a police report and found herself and her children a safe place. But it was very hard to break free, she said. Why? She mentioned several relational manipulations common to abusers. "He kept me confused, lied to me, and blamed me for everything."

This listener grew so full of self-doubt that she ultimately wondered if she was going crazy. This is not an uncommon theme in homes where domestic violence is present. The main characteristic seen in domestic violence situations is an imbalance of power and control through intimidation. A harsh look or gesture can do this. Sometimes isolation is the preferred path. Controlling what she does, who she sees, and where she goes is a common tactic. Emotional abuse as well as economic abuse can keep a woman from getting help. If she doesn't have any money at her disposal, doesn't have a job, is constantly put down, or is called names, her internal resources are so depleted often all she can do is try to survive the situation. Not all abuse is the same, and it might differ from time to time in intensity and gravity, but when someone is using coercion or threats, or possibly male privilege, then you have a gross imbalance of power and control.

Abuse can happen at all ages and stages. I was recently made aware of a husband turned abusive as a result of aging and Alzheimer's. As our population ages, stories of abused seniors hit home. A friend told me of a widowed senior who remarried in her sixties only to find that her new husband was abusive.

JESUS STOPS A POWER PLAY

I believe one of the messages that women need to hear loud and clear, above all other messages, is that Jesus loves women. The Hagar story addressed "God sees women." Here we cover "Jesus loves women."

Come with me and take a look at a New Testament story that involves violence against a woman. You're probably familiar with this story from John 8. Jesus is teaching in the temple and the teachers of the Law and the Pharisees bring in a woman caught in adultery. "In the Law Moses commanded us to stone such women. Now what do you say?" (v. 5). Their main goal is to trip Jesus up. They are hoping to trap him, to find a reason to accuse him.

Jesus bends down and writes in the dust while still being questioned by the crowd. He stands up and says, "Let any one of you who is without sin be the first to throw a stone at her" (v. 7 TNIV). And as he stoops down to write in the sand again, the accusers begin to walk away, one by one. "Woman, where are they? Has no one condemned you?" Jesus asks (v. 10).

"No one, sir," she says.

"Then neither do I condemn you," Jesus declares. "Go now and leave your life of sin" (v. 11).

This poor woman was dragged into the temple and humiliated. If she was "caught in the act," where was the man? Evidently the religious leaders weren't interested in dragging *him* to the temple. She was likely set up so they would have a difficult scenario to present to Jesus.

I've always wondered how the woman felt. Even if she was sleeping around, which the text doesn't deny, she is still someone of value, made by God for his purposes. She wasn't junk. She didn't deserve to be treated as such no matter what decisions she made. Even though the Pharisees were willing to sacrifice her in order to make a point, she was someone who mattered to God. So we have this face-off. Pharisees and religious leaders versus Jesus. Jesus was in a no-win situation, and a bunch of men were standing around ogling this woman, who was very possibly naked, or scantily clad at best.

There are all kinds of speculations about what Jesus bent down to write in the sand. In his commentary on the gospel of John, William Barclay offers an interesting possibility. "It might well be that the leering, lustful look on the faces of the Scribes and Pharisees, the bleak cruelty in their eyes, the prurient curiosity of the crowd, the shame of the woman, all combined to twist the very heart of Jesus in agony and pity, so that He hid His eyes."[3] At the least Jesus tries to draw attention away from the woman. With eyes on him maybe she could get what little clothing she had on readjusted, take a breath, close her eyes, get back whatever dignity she had left. I think Jesus was rushing to her side by doodling in the dirt.

Erwin and Rebecca Lutzer say, "We are struck by the contrast between these men and Jesus. They were full of unholy excitement, passionate about their accusation, anxious to catch Him in a trap. Jesus, on the other hand, was calm and composed and full of compassion rather than condemnation."[4]

As in this story, Jesus often tells those in power to get over themselves and tells the powerless to get up and find their voice. He challenges the bullies and sides with those on the margins of culture, even a woman caught in sin who is being used as a pawn in a silly game of trying to trip up Jesus.

Erwin and Rebecca Lutzer suggest, "This story is usually called, 'Jesus and the Adulterous Woman,' but actually it could be titled, 'Jesus and the Adulterous Men.' "[5] When Jesus tells the religious leaders and Pharisees that whoever is without sin should cast the first stone, it doesn't take long for the crowd to disperse. As each runs through a mental inventory of his immorality, footsteps are heard leaving the temple area.

Jesus then turns to the woman and with love and compassion, along with forgiveness, helps her put her past behind her as he says, "Go now and leave your life of sin."

A BIBLICAL LOOK AT DOMESTIC VIOLENCE

Jesus demonstrates in the Gospels over and over again that he loves women, that he values women highly. (Try reading the story of the Samaritan woman in John 4.) How are we to value women today? How do we look at domestic violence biblically?

I received an email from a woman who grew up in an abusive "Christian" home. The daughter, though emotionally scarred, could eventually leave home, but she had grave concerns for her mother, who seemed to think God wanted her to put up with the violence. When and because the daughter threatened to tell the church about her father's abuse, her parents went and talked to the pastor. His response? "My home pastor just told them to read the Bible more." As for the father? "Ironically, he doesn't believe he has done anything wrong."

In case there is any question that it could possibly be all right to show violence toward women, let me point us to some very directive Scriptures. For starters, consider Colossians 3:19, "Husbands, love your wives and do not be harsh with them." This is a statement where Scripture leaves no room for arguing. Ephesians 5:25–28 takes this attitude further: "Husbands, love your wives, just as Christ loved the church and gave himself up for her to make her holy, cleansing her by the washing with water through the word, and to present her to himself as a radiant church, without stain or wrinkle or any other blemish, but holy and blameless. In this same way, husbands ought to love their wives as their own bodies. He who loves his wife loves himself."

This is beyond just loving and caring for someone. This is a sacrificial love, the kind of love where you lay down your life for someone. This is the love a husband is called to exhibit toward his wife.

After I read *A Thousand Splendid Suns*, I decided to read more Middle Eastern literature that might enlighten me on the treatment of women, especially in the Muslim culture. I read *Reading Lolita in Tehran* and *Kabul Beauty School*, as well as the controversial book *Infidel*. The Qur'an speaks of the treatment of women in the following way. Contrast this with what Scripture says.

In Sura 4:34 we read, "The men are made responsible for the women, and GOD has endowed them with certain qualities, and made them the bread earners. The righteous women will cheerfully accept this arrangement, since it is GOD's commandment, and honor their husbands during their absence. If you experience rebellion from the women, you shall first talk to them, then (*you may use negative incentives like*) deserting them in bed, then you may (*as a last alternative*) beat them. If they obey you, you are not permitted to transgress against them."[6] In the Muslim world it is allowable to do harm to women, even beat them, if they are disobedient.

On Friday evening in observant Jewish homes, part of the Jewish Sabbath ritual is to read the last twenty-two verses from Proverbs 31. It is called Eshet Chayil in Hebrew, meaning Woman of Valor. This hymn is recited by the men before sitting down to the Shabbat evening meal. As a Jewish man recites this Scripture passage, he is reminded of all his wife has done for him and the household over the course of the previous week. The recitation from Proverbs 31 every week demonstrates this culture's high view of women.

Why are we so cautious about helping a woman step out of a situation where she is experiencing violence? "I don't want to look like I'm condoning divorce." This is one reason given, and often the reason why churches don't support organizations that stand up for women encountering violence. People often cite Malachi 2:16, which reads, " 'I hate divorce,' says the Lord God of Israel." They don't seem to notice or quote the rest of the very same verse, the very same sentence: " '... and I hate a man's covering himself with violence as well as with his garment,' says the Lord Almighty." Psalm 11:5 is a great capstone to this topic: "The Lord examines the righteous, but the wicked, those who love violence, he hates with a passion" (TNIV).

A woman living daily with domestic violence will struggle with leaving the situation. And sometimes the church makes it harder for her because we keep bringing up religious ideas that perpetuate abuse. Often Genesis 3 is part of this discussion. What we have to remember about the Genesis passage that focuses on the fall and its consequence is that the conditions that result are due to human disobedience. This was not God's original plan. He had good intentions for us. He did not intend for there to be pain in childbirth, or for husbands to rule over their wives (Genesis 3:16). Neither did he desire there to be painful toil and thistles and weeds in the fields of labor for the man (vv. 17 – 19).

We also look at the fact that we are no longer under judgment because of Christ's sacrifice. We are, as believers in Christ, new creations, living by the power of the Holy Spirit. These judgments rendered in Genesis 3 can be redeemed, are *intended* to be redeemed. For some reason many in the church are still living under these judgments, and as such are grieving the very heart of God. Craig S. Keener writes, "God never intended for such relationships [marriages] to be a powerplay; that was introduced into the world by sin."[7]

How should we respond to violence? What is the biblical

response? It is good to protect yourself from violent people. Matthew 5:39, "But I tell you, do not resist an evil person. If anyone slaps you on the right cheek, turn to them the other cheek also" (TNIV), is often quoted to encourage a woman to stay in her violent scenario. With further study it is evident that the idea isn't to "take it" when you are continually punished, but rather not to be violent in return; to actually *avoid* further encounters is the intent here. Proverbs 27:12 says, "The prudent see danger and take refuge, but the simple keep going and suffer for it." Ephesians 5:11 says, "Have nothing to do with the fruitless deeds of darkness, but rather expose them." There is a time to heed Paul's exhortation in Ephesians 4:15, to speak the truth in love, and also Ephesians 4:25 cannot be missed: "Therefore each of you must put off falsehood and speak truthfully to your neighbor, for we are all members of one body" (TNIV). Proverbs 19:19 reads, "The hot-tempered must pay the penalty; rescue them, and you will have to do it again" (TNIV).

If a friend approached you to tell you she's in an abusive relationship, what would you do? It's one thing to know what Scripture says, and to understand that the church hasn't stepped up its game, but what would *you* do?

First, ask her if she feels in imminent danger. If not, then explore the kind of abuse being perpetrated against her. Encourage her to get counseling just for her. Find out if her spouse is willing to go to marital counseling. Help your friend find a suitable counselor through a trusted domestic violence network. Contact the abuse hotline listed on page 203. Most pastors are not equipped to counsel in this type of situation.

If your friend is directly in danger, help her find a safe place to go. At the least, encourage her to keep a duplicate set of keys for car and house, a change of clothes, and copies of important papers with you or another friend so she can access them if she has to flee quickly. It usually takes a victim of domestic violence six or seven times to leave the situation permanently. If you are her friend, be patient and don't lose heart. Keep supporting her and praying for her, because she is living in a situation filled with chaos, fear, and uncertainty.

I am reminded of one more biblical story—of childless Hannah, who was tormented not by a husband but by another woman in the household. It is reminiscent of the story of Sarai and Hagar, but when Hannah sought help for her pain—her barrenness as well as her abuse—her trouble was dismissed by the local priest Eli. The priest not only dismissed her pain but even accused her of being drunk. Hannah courageously held her ground: "No, my lord, I am a woman troubled in spirit. I have drunk neither wine nor strong drink, but I have been pouring out my soul before the Lord." Now listen to this. She continues: "Do not regard your servant as a worthless woman, for all along I have been speaking out of my great anxiety and vexation" (1 Samuel 1:15–16 ESV). Eli then recognized her truth and replied, "Go in peace, and the God of Israel grant your petition that you have made to him" (v. 17 ESV).

This is not a book about how to reform the church. And this is a difficult issue that many church leaders don't understand and are afraid to touch. In conservative evangelical circles we hold the Word of God in high regard, as we should. But we often hold the Word of God in one hand and compassion in the other and have trouble bringing our two hands together. It seems we ask the WWJD (What Would Jesus Do) question in almost every circumstance except domestic violence. As Christ followers, can we sit back and not act to support and help the woman who finds herself experiencing domestic violence? This may involve some additional education on the subject. Many helpful resources are available today for further reading and training on this topic. If we are to be the body of Christ, we cannot ignore what Jesus did not.

DISCUSSION QUESTIONS

1. What has been your experience with domestic violence? Have you ever known anyone who has lived with this?

2. If you are involved in a situation where you feel threatened, have you told anyone? What steps are you taking to provide safety for yourself and others you love?

3. Has the issue of domestic violence arisen in your church and been dealt with well? And if it hasn't arisen, is it a signal that women are afraid to bring it up? Why do you think the church is often afraid of tackling the issue of domestic violence?

4. As a church body, what steps do you need to take to address domestic violence when the issue arises?

5. If you were approached by a friend who tells you she is in an abusive relationship, what would you do?

6. How does Jesus see women and love women? If you struggle believing that you are seen and loved by God, what can you do to move toward understanding his love for you?

chapter five

NEVER ENOUGH

What Women Tell Me:
  My husband has looked at porn since he was a little kid. We naively thought he could quit if we got married.

• • •

MY SON AND I HAD JUST returned from a quick Christmas trip to visit my parents in Florida. On a cold Chicago January night, after I'd put John to bed, I wanted to have a fire—a gas fire with ceramic logs—in the fireplace. But for some reason it wouldn't light. I figured the gas had been turned off, so I decided to follow the gas line from the point where it went down into the basement. I hoped that if I traced the right pipe, I'd find the proper valve to turn on.

So I started following some copper pipes. The next thing I knew, I had lost those pipes and was following the heating duct. As I followed the heating duct, I spotted something sticking out over the edge, on top of the duct. A small stepladder leaned against the wall right there next to me, so I opened it and climbed up to see what I had spotted. What I found made me want to vomit. It was a stack of hard-core pornographic videos.

I started shaking uncontrollably as my mind raced. Did these belong to the man I was married to? How would I confront him about this? My gut said the videos were his. I felt paralyzed, confused, afraid, and betrayed. What should I do now? Should I ignore this and hope it would go away?

The usual reaction to trauma is either fight or flight, but a third reaction was my biggest temptation in that moment: denial and inaction. I sensed God telling me to put the videos back. So I did. I also put the stepladder back against the wall and walked up the stairs in a daze, trying to figure out what to do.

That was the beginning of a three-year journey that, unfortunately, ended in divorce. The details aren't all that important, but I am here to tell you that if you've discovered the same secret in your marriage, you might feel like your world has imploded, like the relationship you thought you had was a sham. The truth is the world as you know it has dramatically changed, but every good moment you have experienced in your marriage up until now wasn't a lie, and God is with you even now, and he is in control. His heart is hurting, and he is weeping right along with you.

I have often been reminded through my son that God is a redeeming God. I can look at John and know this past relationship had some real high points, and he was the pinnacle. Because of the journey God has taken me on, today I can actually say that the best thing that ever happened to me was marrying my ex-husband. I had to travel a long mud-covered road to get there, but God continues to redeem my past. I can also say that Jesus took off his sandals and stepped into the mud and walked with me.

STARTLING STATISTICS

It's easy to understand why one listener says, "My stomach gets in knots when I hear this subject come up." I know sexual addiction is not just a men's issue. Sexual addiction in women is on the rise largely due to our highly sexualized and visual culture. In fact, according to internet-filter-review.com, 28 percent of those admitting to sexual addiction are women. However, I am only going to address the side of the issue that I hear about so often from *Midday Connection* listeners: how to survive in a marriage when your husband is a sexual addict.

ComScore Media Metrix reports that 70 percent of men ages eighteen to thirty-four visit a pornographic site in a typical month. As the mother of a son, this frighten me. When a friend, whose son attends a Christian school, told me of boys passing around porn images on their cell phones on the school bus, my heart sank. There is pornography-blocking software for PCs, there are mechanisms to block programs on cable networks, but what do you do when someone else passes porn to your child on a school bus?

A 2001 *Christianity Today* survey showed 33 percent of clergy admitted to having visited a sexually explicit website. Of those who had visited a porn site, 53 percent had visited those sites a few times in the past year, and 18 percent visit sexually explicit sites between a couple of times a month and more than once a week.[1] A *Leadership Journal* survey on Christians and sex[2] reported 57 percent of pastors say that addiction to pornography is the most sexually damaging issue in their congregation.

I believe pornography addiction may be the number one tool of the enemy in our world today, and yes, even in our churches. Satan is waging war on the hearts and minds of our men, and we need to storm the gates of heaven in prayer for our men and for our boys. I believe that more than ever before.

RATIONALIZING

When confronted with their husbands' secret sexual lives, women often try to rationalize the unacceptable activity. "Well, he wasn't with an actual person; he wasn't sleeping with a prostitute—he was only looking at magazines and videos."

Some people ask, "Isn't every man into viewing porn, at least a little? Boys will be boys. Isn't it okay to indulge a little?" But porn degrades you as a woman made in the image of God. A husband who views porn has been giving himself away to other women, having sex without you, his wife. Jesus said in Matthew 5:27–28, "You have heard that it was said, 'Do not commit adultery.' But I tell you that anyone who looks at a woman lustfully has already committed adultery with her in his heart." Jesus is saying no, the secret sin is not okay.

In her book *Is There Really Sex after Kids?* Jill Savage describes the effect of pornography by comparing it to "a siren in Greek mythology who lured sailors to their deaths on rocky coasts with her seductive singing." She continues, "Pornography lures men to their basements, their laptops, and their PCs resulting in emotional death and the death of marital intimacy. The voice that calls them is that of the enemy who whispers the lies of sex without the responsibilities of relationship. It is a dead end street."[3]

To use another metaphor: As I'm writing this we are under a severe thunderstorm warning, with the possibility of heavy hail. It's a great picture of the climate in the home when secrets are discovered. Lightning can strike with little notice, and you are always waiting and watching for the hailstorm. Fear is the underlying emotion that follows you around, and you just don't know what to do.

When reality sets in—that "something is rotten in Denmark," as Shakespeare said in *Hamlet*—there certainly is a deep sense of betrayal. If that's what you are feeling, it is usually profound and definitely real. I remember praying, "I wish I hadn't made this discovery, Lord. I'd rather go back to living without knowing." Muddling through life with a sickly marriage seemed like a better option than addressing the problem head-on. God, however, didn't think so. After seeing a counselor, I knew I had to confront the situation.

THE ADDICTIVE CYCLE

When I use the term "sexual addict," I'm talking about someone who cannot control his or her relationship to sexual stimulation. There's a "never enough" driving compulsion that when acted on can become habitual, even central to his life. It's not unlike drug or alcohol addiction, where a mood-altering chemical is used. Brain chemicals accompanying sexual release, either with another individual or through masturbation, provide a mood-altering experience. As with the drug or alcohol addict, there is a progression that takes the sexual addict deeper into the secret addiction and further from friends and family. Because of the nature of this secret, shame-filled life, when the addict is "found out," the denial can run very deep.

Sometimes if he's been caught at the very beginning of the slippery slope, this jolt may be exactly what he needs to move him forward in dealing with what might have developed into a serious addiction.

One thing experts agree on is the repetitive, cyclical nature of sexual addiction. The following page shows a picture of the addictive system from Patrick Carnes's book *Out of the Shadows*.[4]

I've heard from women with a sexually addicted spouse that they can almost see this cycle at work. "He'll start to distance himself from me. I know he struggles with self-esteem. He can't believe that I really love him." You can see how someone with a

THE ADDICTIVE SYSTEM

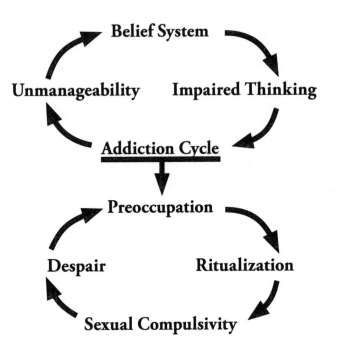

faulty belief system moves into impaired thinking, and then the addiction cycle begins. The addict starts to become preoccupied with what will ease the pain of his feelings of worthlessness. Patrick Carnes puts forth that the sexual experience is a means for maintaining emotional balance, because everything else in the addict's life feels out of balance. Sexual addicts are noted for being moody, partly because after the sexually compulsive part of the cycle come great feelings of despair. And that is actually what kicks the addict back to the false beliefs. "I am worthless. I have to do something to make myself feel better." And on and on the cycle goes. Once a woman knows she is living with an addict and understands the addictive system, she can often spot the progress of the addict in the cycle.

Sexual addiction visually stimulated by pornography does not always progress to another level. Even so, it can become such a stumbling block to normal living that it can lead to job loss because of the inordinate amount of time spent viewing Internet porn at work or viewing on- demand porn movies in hotels while on business trips. I've seen families saddled with huge credit card debt because of the money the addict spent buying videos and magazines. If this kind of stimulation ceases to satisfy, the addict can move on to voyeurism, exposing, or sex for hire. Then the addiction can move even further into deviant behavior.

Masturbation can become so much the norm that to have sex with a real person sometimes doesn't even hold appeal for the sexual addict. For example, an addict can become so sore from compulsive masturbating that he can't perform with his wife due to the pain. Many think that sexual addiction means the addict wants sex all the time with his wife. And while that may be true in some cases, more often the opposite is true, and sex becomes so infrequent that you are left confused, fearing something is wrong with you as a woman and wife.

Unless a man tells you he has a problem with porn, many men marry believing marriage will be the antidote to their addiction. Their wife-to-be is none the wiser, because usually the addict can table the addiction for a period of time, and the soon-to-be Mrs. becomes the muse for a short time until the knot is tied and the addictive cycle begins again.

SOMETHING'S NOT RIGHT

Before I found my husband's pornography, I had known for a number of years that something was not right, at least on one level. I couldn't put my finger on it, but I lived with regular unease. In his book *Out of the Shadows*, Patrick Carnes says, "The myth is that the family does not know about the secret sexual life. Yet, at one level, they always do know ... even the children."[5] As I look back, I know that to be true.

An addictive pattern draws individuals emotionally away from their loved ones. They work to withhold themselves and they don't trust anyone, sometimes especially their own families. This is a deeply felt pain both for the addict and for the spouse. As a spouse you cannot help but sense the distance, and as the addiction increases so does the distance. Reacting to my husband's distrust, I became more isolated. I remember when I was on maternity leave. As a typical mom, I was going stir crazy and needed some adult time. I would make arrangements to meet other mothers with infants from church when my husband would be away at work. When he would call, I remember talking as if I were sitting at home in our living room, so he wouldn't know I was out with friends. I knew he wouldn't be happy but couldn't put my finger on why. In some ways his pain became my pain.

Yes, the addict is a person in pain, and the addiction is what numbs him to that pain and helps him escape having to feel his true feelings. Most of us don't relish dealing with difficult feelings. We sometimes choose not to address them and then find ourselves actually dying a slow emotional death. It's counterintuitive really. The healing comes when we address the pain head-on instead of avoiding it. Because of the isolating nature of addiction, when an addict finds himself in the middle of his deepest need, he also finds himself cut off from anyone who can help.

Here's a picture of this in the physical realm that might be helpful. My maternal grandfather, a farmer in northern Maine, was a wonderful man. He had a small, fifty-acre farm where he grew all kinds of vegetables and some fruits. I've never seen a harder-working man. He was one of nineteen children and only made it through the eighth grade. The way to survive in his world was to work, and to work hard. So when he experienced some physical symptoms that might have pointed toward illness, he ignored them. He didn't have time for that. It was planting season, then it was harvest season, then it was winter and he had to head to Florida to be the head baker in a resort hotel so there would be money to buy seed for planting season, and so on. It was never the right time to address the real problem. It was easier to live in denial until denial took him straight to the hospital, where he eventually died of colon cancer. He died because he wouldn't address the problem before it became fatal.

I've seen many marriages die, including mine, because the real problem wasn't addressed soon enough. We get especially afraid when the addiction is sexual addiction, because our sexuality is such an integral part of us, linked directly to our person. It is the most intimate part of who we are.

A *Midday* listener who took pride in keeping herself attractive, exciting, and available for her husband discovered that her husband was viewing Internet pornography almost daily. She confronted him, and he claimed he'd "dealt with it." Yet she desperately asks, "How can I get past the lie? Why am I not enough?" That question strikes at the very core of who a woman is. We already feel like we are "less than," having bought in to so many cultural lies, and if you are in a marriage with a sexual addict, you know that you are not enough. You cannot satisfy him, which translates to "You aren't beautiful enough, sexy enough, and you are a failure at the fundamental level of your feminine self."

Here's some good news. That is not true! But because your spouse has a faulty belief system, it begins to affect your core beliefs as well, and the healthier one in the relationship often becomes the co-addict. Significant healing does have to take place to move you to the point where you stop believing the lies. Satan's lies. Your spouse's lies. The lies you tell yourself.

THE CO-ADDICT

I've grappled with why I was drawn to an addict, and I've seen, in my case, it takes one to know one. I struggled with self-esteem issues before I married, and being in relationship with an addict intensified those feelings of worthlessness. I was a true co-addict as often is the case when one is married to an addict. And it might be helpful for you to do some reading and learning about the codependent nature of a person married to an addict. At some point in the marriage, I started on my own addictive cycle and began using food to soothe and nurture myself. I would feel bad about the amount of food I ate, or the weight I gained, but then I needed to soothe how I felt about that, and the cycle began again. Most addictions have a similar cycle. I unconsciously made allowances for his addiction as I needed room for my own. Food was my way of coping.

On one level, really, all of us are addicts. We all love something too much and think that thing will make our lives better, but it ends up making our lives worse, sometimes much worse. I equate it to the days when my son, John, was four or five and he'd latch onto a new video and watch it over and over and over and over, and did I say he watched it over and over? It was the compulsive nature of a little kid. As a parent, I couldn't let him continue down that path of compulsive behavior. It wasn't good for him.

As adults we usually know when something is unhealthy for us. But when we suffer with an emotional or physical addiction, there is a compulsive component that makes the addiction impossible to shake in our own power. But we can get the help we need, the healing God offers.

WOULD YOU LIKE TO GET WELL?

John 5 tells an incredibly interesting story of Jesus healing a man who had been sick for thirty-eight years. It's layered with relevance for anyone with addictions. It seems that for many of those years, this debilitated man had been lying beside the pool of Bethesda. Apparently the pool had some healing properties, so that when the water stirred, sick people rushed to catch the benefit of the bubbling spring. Scripture says that Jesus saw this man, discerned the length and severity of his illness, and then asked a startling question: "Would you like to get well?"

What? I would have assumed that the man wanted to get well. Doesn't everyone who is sick want to get well? If I've learned one thing so far in my life, it's "never assume."

The gospel's narrative indicates that the man never answered Jesus' question. He gave an excuse. "I can't." Why? "I have no one to put me into the pool when the water bubbles up. Someone else always gets there ahead of me." As I see it, this man whined to Jesus. Okay, I've done my fair share of whining to Jesus, but here's what raises a red flag for me: The man had been there thirty-eight years and didn't know anyone well enough who could help him into the pool? Talk about an isolated life.

I propose this man was afraid to be made well. He was afraid to leave the life he had known. On the surface, he probably did want to get better, but he had become dependent on a beggar's lifestyle. People would toss him a coin now and then, and a scrap of food, enough to get by. It wasn't the best life, but it was his life, a life he had become comfortable with. He reminds me of someone struggling with an addiction. The Amplified Version of the Bible describes the man as someone who suffered with a deep-seated and lingering disorder; as the story goes on, we see that it's a disorder of both body and soul.

I think most addicts give lip service to wanting change,

but deep down they are scared to death of what that change might mean. They fear the pain that has to be addressed. They fear being abandoned by those they love. Once the truth has surfaced, it is overwhelming. They can't imagine how they can make it without running back to their addiction.

Jesus responded with a command: "Get up! Pick up your mat, and walk" (v. 8), and the man was healed. He picked up his mat and walked. But that's not the end of the story. Jesus had healed the man on the Sabbath, which rankled the Pharisees. Because Jesus had left the scene, they confronted the healed man: "It is the Sabbath; the law forbids you to carry your mat" (v. 10).

The story takes another curious turn: "Later Jesus found him at the temple and said to him, 'See, you are well again. Stop sinning or something worse may happen to you'" (v. 14). Evidently the man is sinning when Jesus finds him in the temple. We don't know exactly what he is doing, but we could guess that he's gone back to what he knows, back to what feels good, what feels comfortable. Maybe he was begging, pretending to still be lame. He might have been physically healed, but it appears that his heart has not changed.

The heart is the key component to any life transformation. No heart change, no life change. Our human, sinful nature will always lead us back to the dung pile, back to the addiction, back to the sin, back to the comfortable. We need the Holy Spirit of God at work in us to give us the power to move forward, one small step at a time.

WAITING FOR A RESPONSE

In the aftermath of my discovery of the pornography, I came to understand and cling to the truth of Galatians 4:4: "But when the time had fully come, God sent his Son." To say God's timing is always right is so cliché, but I saw time after time that I would not have been ready to stand, to fight, to resist, to press on until the fullness of time. It's as if a spiritual and emotional gestation had to occur before God allowed me to know certain things. It was certainly one way that I saw he was in total control of my situation, even if I felt out of control. The waiting was the hard part. When you're dealing with sexual addiction, there is a lot of waiting. You wait to see if the addict will admit to the addiction. You wait to see if the addict will choose help and healing. You wait to see if today will be a day of sobriety.

More than one counselor told me, "Time is on your side." But waiting is so difficult, especially relational waiting. A recurring theme among listener emails has to do with trust: "How do I trust that he isn't hiding it again?" Or "Anytime he has access to a computer at all, I get nervous." For most women, and I'm no exception, if there is relational unrest, we find it hard to concentrate on anything until resolution takes place. Sometimes that is just not possible, and we have to lean into God like we never have before. Did things move quickly? Were my prayers answered overnight? Were my prayers answered in the ways I wanted? No, no, and no. But I cried out to God, and his answers came, and his answers were better than what I had requested.

Cry out to God; he can take it. I would drive in to work at Moody Radio, literally screaming out to God in my car. My car became my sanctuary. Find a personal sanctuary like that. Dig into the Psalms and scream them out to God. Psalm 6 and Psalm 13 are good ones to start with. I cried out Psalm 6:6–9 on many occasions.

> *I am worn out from groaning;*
>   *all night long I flood my bed with weeping*
>   *and drench my couch with tears.*
> *My eyes grow weak with sorrow;*
>   *they fail because of all my foes.*

Away from me, all you who do evil,
*   for the LORD has heard my weeping.*
The LORD has heard my cry for mercy;
*   the LORD accepts my prayer.*

Psalm 13:1–2 also got a workout in my car sanctuary.

How long, O LORD? Will you forget me forever?
*   How long will you hide your face from me?*
How long must I wrestle with my thoughts
*   and every day have sorrow in my heart?*
*   How long will my enemy triumph over me?*

It is powerful to pray the words of Scripture back to God. He does hear our prayers. I'm convinced that God loved me much and knew I wouldn't draw closer to him until crisis hit my life, and that's why I discovered the stash of pornography that January night.

I've been a Christ follower for years, but I didn't know God deeply. When my life came crashing down, I had no choice but to get to know him. I prayed a certain prayer over and over during this time in my life. I first heard this Larry Crabb prayer when he used it in one of his messages at a Moody Bible Institute Founder's Week Bible Conference. It became the prayer of my life. "Lord, I know you're all that I have, but I don't know you well enough for you to be all that I need." I knew that was true of me, and I was desperate for Jesus to come and wrap his arms around me and walk with me through this mess. I sure didn't know how to unravel it. Jesus did, but in the process I had to learn the spiritual gift of waiting.

HELP AND HOPE

I know what you're asking. Is there any hope? I say a resounding yes! Will the road be difficult and filled with challenges? I say again a resounding yes! Can God work in willing hearts, both yours and your spouse's? Another resounding yes! Discovering your spouse is a sexual addict is not the end of the story. There can be confession and repentance, as with any sin. But with any addiction, or any sin that has a gripping hold on us, it is often three steps forward, two steps back. So how do you move forward if you're married to a sexual addict? Each situation is a little different, but some foundational principles are the same. Here are some steps I advise you to take.

Insist your husband see a counselor. It is best if you can find an expert in sexual addiction, but at the least someone experienced in the field of addictions. This is not a counseling job for your pastor. As much as I love my pastor, and pastors in general—hey, I'm a pastor's kid—they aren't usually equipped for counseling in the field of addictions.

Find a good counselor for you. You are trying to hold your own world together. You might be working full-time or be a full-time mom, and you need emotional help and support. I would have crumbled without my counselor. You may be going with your husband to his counselor at times too, but you need your own counselor. I can hear you saying, "We don't have the money." If you need to go to your church and ask for financial help to cover this, then please do. If you need to ask a friend for some financial help for a time, then please do. See if your insurance will cover the counseling. Sometimes it will, especially if it's for an addiction or seen as family counseling. This varies depending on your insurance plan and the state in which you live.

Set some boundaries for the journey ahead. Your counselor will help you with this. If you are unfamiliar with the concept of boundaries, here's a good definition: "Simply put, a boundary is your personal 'property line.' It defines who you are, where you end, and where others begin. It refers to the truth, to reality, to what is. When you confront someone about a problem, you are setting a boundary. You can set a boundary with your words when you are honest and when you establish a consequence for another's hurtful actions."[6]

Block pornography from your computers. There are helpful filtering and blocking programs that you can install on your computer that can keep your spouse and children safe from intentional or inadvertent porn viewing. Learn how to check the history on your computer, which is simply checking to see what websites your family members are frequenting. If your husband says your family doesn't need software like this, tell him this is a nonnegotiable for you.

Find a friend or confidant you can tell about your spouse's addiction. I know often the wife of the addict has been somewhat isolated and may not have close friends. I had to take some risks when I found out about my husband's addiction. Before divulging your personal situation, you need to state the confidential nature of what you are about to share, and you might test the waters with a smaller confidence for a week or two just to make sure you are relating with someone who can hold her tongue. I went to my neighbor Faith and asked her if we could talk. She opened her door and invited me in, and I'm sure she had no idea how her life would change as a result. She signed on to journey with me, and I wouldn't be writing this chapter today if Faith hadn't been a solid rock in my world during those dark days.

Get tested for HIV/AIDS. I recently heard about a woman who discovered she had contracted a sexually transmitted disease and then found out her husband had been with prostitutes and other partners — for who knows how long. Getting tested for HIV was the loneliest moment of my life, bar none.

I remember not wanting to tell anyone, even those friends who knew the situation, because I felt it was so humiliating to have to be tested. It put the reality of the situation right in my face. I went to the test alone and then went out to lunch alone. If I had it to do over, I would have taken a friend, which is what I recommend you do.

The possibility exists that both you and your spouse can become "wounded healers," to use Henri Nouwen's phrase. Another possible reality is that your spouse may not choose to walk a path toward freedom and wholeness. If your spouse does not choose this road of healing and recovery, you can still choose this path for yourself, and God will give you the strength. It will take the support of good friends and the help of a good counselor. If your spouse doesn't choose recovery, eventually a fork in the road will come. Do you continue on in the marriage, or do you walk the difficult road of divorce? Sometimes that choice is made for you, but more often than not the pathology of an addict also includes fear of abandonment and the difficult decision may be left solely to you.

No one can answer these questions for you, and there is much to weigh as you contemplate the answers. God's heart is for you to be safe. If there is physical, emotional, or verbal abuse emanating from your spouse, then your safety as well as the safety of your children, if they are still in the home, must be your primary concern. God desires for your marriage to be whole and healed, but in the end, God cares more for you as an individual than he does the institution of marriage. Health for you and your children apart from your sick spouse may be the wiser path. There are no easy answers, but let me again say that God will give you the strength and support you need for the path he leads you down.

DISCUSSION QUESTIONS

1. What has been your experience with sexual addiction or pornography? Have you ever known anyone who has lived through this?

2. Has your church or pastor dealt adequately with the issue of pornography use? If not, why? How could the local church address this issue?

3. How can you personally address this issue in your own life or family?

4. If you were approached by a friend who tells you she is struggling with sexual addiction or a sexually addicted husband, what would you do?

chapter six

SINGLE WITH CHILDREN

What Women Tell Me:
We hear how couples with two incomes "struggle"—without them stopping to try to imagine what our situation might be and offer a helping hand.

•••

HIS SEVEN-YEAR-OLD BEDTIME PRAYERS BROKE MY heart. He wanted me to go on the field trip so badly, but I wasn't a room mom. I don't know about your school district, but here only room moms were allowed to accompany a class on field trips—unless one of the room moms had to cancel, in which case the teacher needed to find a substitute.

I couldn't possibly sign up to be a room mom. Like so many other single moms, I had to work full-time. But when I heard John's prayers, I promised him I'd call his teacher to get on a waiting list for the Brookfield Zoo field trip in case someone canceled. I acted on my promise and left a message with Mrs. Weglarz. Actually, I left three different voice mail messages but heard nothing. I remember being a little irritated. "At least she could call me back to let me know if there is a slight possibility." Exercising what little faith I had—on John's behalf—I'd even arranged to take the day off of work.

Just after dinner on the night before the field trip, I decided to run to the grocery store. For single moms with young children, one of the most difficult things to do is go shopping, especially grocery shopping. You rarely get to go without your kids. The looming question is always, "How young is too young to leave them home alone?" Trust me, if you're a single mom, you've probably made the midnight grocery store run just so you could go alone. Or at least you've thought about doing it. You can accomplish twice as much in half the time when you're alone. In my case the grocery store was less than a block away from my home. Grateful for its proximity and entrusting my son to the VCR, I ran to the store. "I'll be back before the video is over," I told him.

Anytime a single mom goes anywhere alone it's a treat, even the grocery store. Tonight it didn't feel that way, though. My heart was aching for John, who had poured his heart out to God about me going on his field trip. He wanted to feel like all the other kids whose moms stepped up to the plate.

On my way to the store, I prayed the typical mom prayer, trying to save face for God, as if he didn't know what was going on. "God, I don't care about me. I understand how this world works, how complicated things can be, but I'm talking about a little boy here, who really believes in you, who thinks you can work miracles. I mean, I know that stuff really doesn't happen, but he doesn't know that yet." It was a pathetic prayer that really showed the extent of my small view of God. And showed that on that particular day I had forgotten a long line of blessings I'd already received. But you know that tenacious mother love. You can mess with me, but you'd better not mess with my kid. In all actuality it was idolatry, but that was the posture I was taking with God on this issue. Asking nicely wasn't working, so I decided to try to manipulate God.

I don't even remember what I needed at the store, what was so urgent that I had to leave John home alone. I came to the potato chip aisle and decided a nice bag of salty goodness would drown out my sadness. I turned up the aisle, and just about midway I moved to the side to make room for another woman shopping alone. I looked up, startled to see John's first grade teacher, Mrs. Weglarz. "What are you doing here?" I asked.

"Oh, I never shop at this store, but my kids are at piano lessons around the corner, and I thought I had just enough time to run in and grab a few things before I pick them up."

I was just about to ask her how plans were going for the field trip and if she got my messages, when she said, "I'm so glad I saw you tonight. I've been calling and calling your number, and I keep getting a message that says your phone number is out of service." I had completely forgotten that in the throes of my divorce, I had changed our home phone number but hadn't given the new number to the school. Mrs. Weglarz had indeed had a room mom cancel, and she was hoping that I could go even with this last-minute notice. "I realize you've called several times, but I rarely check my voice mail at school. I didn't get your messages until today."

You won't be surprised at my answer: "Yes, I'd love to go."

Not wanting to hold her up or block the aisle any longer, and desperately wanting to get back home to break the news to John, I excused myself and headed for the checkout line. I wasn't sure whether I wanted to laugh or cry, but I fairly floated out of the grocery store. Once in the car, I let the tears flow. I was overwhelmed by God's love and care for a seven-year-old and his thirty-eight-year-old mother.

I rushed in the door and asked John to pause his video. "You'll never guess," I said. John hopped up and down and thought it was, indeed, a miracle. As we hugged, I said, "That's how God works, John. That's just how God works." Even when the grown-up doesn't believe, I had renewed faith that God sees the faith of a child.

The field trip to the zoo was a big success as far as John was concerned. I was assigned six or seven little boys to keep track of. It was an absolute nightmare, constantly counting heads, trying to get them to hold hands, hoping no one slipped through the cracks. I couldn't wait until the day was over and was secretly glad I wasn't a regular room mom. John, however, was happy as a clam, and God, I believe, was smiling.

Not every story had that kind of joyous ending during my five-year stint as a single mom, but enough of those scenarios happened that John got a good picture of who God is and how God works when we trust him and come to him with our needs. So did his mom!

GOD HEARS THE CHILD

We previously looked at the story of Hagar in Genesis 16 and saw that God "sees" an abused woman. We return to the story of Hagar in Genesis 21. Here we see that God hears a child. Hagar birthed Ishmael, and no love was lost between him and his half brother, Isaac, nor Sarah and her maidservant, Hagar. "On the day Isaac was weaned Abraham held a great feast. But Sarah saw that the son whom Hagar the Egyptian had borne to Abraham was mocking, and she said to Abraham, 'Get rid of that slave woman and her son, for that slave woman's son will never share in the inheritance with my son Isaac" (v. 10).

Sarah's pronouncement distressed Abraham, but God assured him he would care for Ishmael. After giving them food and a skin of water, Abraham sent Hagar and Ishmael into the Desert of Beersheba where they wandered. Hagar was a single mom basically turned out onto the street. She was homeless. The water ran out and Hagar believed her son was going to die. She put the boy under a bush and sat a short distance away, thinking, "I can't watch him die." And as she sat there, she began to sob.

God heard the boy crying, and the angel of God called to Hagar, "What is the matter, Hagar? Do not be afraid; God has heard the boy crying as he lies there. Lift the boy up and take him by the hand, for I will make him into a great nation" (Genesis 21:17 – 18). Then God provided her with a well full of water to drink.

I need to hear stories like this one in Genesis 21. In my adult sensibilities I often forget that God hears the heart of a child. He heard the cries of my son, John, just as he heard the cries of Ishmael out in the desert.

WHAT'S THE BIG DEAL?

What kinds of stress do single parents face?

One listener noted her exhaustion at the end of a hard day's work. In the evening she tried not to be impatient with her daughter, and yet ... "When you are at your end and you have no one to hand off your child to, what do you do?"

For me that care issue manifested itself when John got one of his severe migraine headaches. He started getting them at age four, and they would come at the most inopportune times, about three weeks apart, almost like clockwork. Of course he had no control over their arrival. They'd often come in the middle of the night. As a single parent I had to keep watch—alone. Ask any mom who is awakened out of a deep sleep how hard it is to be up with a sick child half the night, then find a caretaker for him the next morning, and still head off to a job and do a full day's work. Those are the times that try single moms' souls.

After one program on single parenting, a mom emailed to say that the key issue for her was poverty. She marveled that her family had survived, especially since she felt she received so little regard or support from others, even in the church. This email was echoed over and over in the *Midday* email box. "Our lives would have been far easier, and we would have felt more loved and accepted, if others had seen our need, and without taking over our lives, had responded."

The level of a mother's education, her ability to get back into the workforce, and the level of child support all affect the financial picture of the single mother caring for children. Bottom line, finances are an issue for a significant number of single mothers.

I too look back and wonder how John and I made it financially. At the end of so many months, I looked at my bank account and sensed that God had performed another "loaves and fishes" for me. He multiplied what I had and there was still something left over. Some of God's provisions were behind the scenes. Some were more dramatic.

One of the perks of *Midday Connection* is having access to some wise Christian women. In the middle of going through my divorce, I had been pouring out my heart to Jan Silvious. She said, "I have a friend in Nashville that you really ought to talk to. It would be worth a trip down there just to meet with her for a day." I sensed that if Jan felt that strongly and was willing to arrange this meeting, I needed to go. My life was in shambles. I had nothing to lose. So I decided to make the trip to Nashville and meet with Jan's friend, Kim Hill, along with Kim's friend Lisa Harper.

Early on the appointed Monday morning, I drove to Midway Airport to catch a cheap Southwest Airlines flight. I arrived in Nashville on time. So far so good. With everything that had been going on in my life to that point, I was happy just to make it that far. Neither Kim nor Lisa could pick me up at the airport, but I knew the name of the restaurant where I was to meet them: the Green Hills Grill. The problem was that I arrived in Nashville with hardly a cent on me, not even money enough for a phone call, not that a phone call would have helped. I had paid for my plane ticket with a credit card. Cash was my main problem. I was living paycheck to paycheck. Legal bills were piling up, counseling bills too, plus John was attending a private Christian school and I didn't want to rip him from the world he knew if I didn't have to, so I tightened my belt and trusted God.

One of the things that plagued me, and I've since learned plagues many women going through a divorce or any traumatic life change, such as being widowed or getting a cancer diagnosis, is what I call brain blackouts. The morning I left for Nashville, it took all the energy I could muster to get John to a friend's house so I could head to the airport for my early flight. Making sure my wallet had cash in it, or that my ride was cared for in Nashville, was the furthest thing from my mind. I was busy arranging a place for John to go after school before my flight returned to Chicago and I could pick him up. At that point in my life, it took almost all my energy to prepare for *Midday Connection* each day. I didn't have a whole lot left, for me or for John.

In the midst of that kind of emotional overload, all kinds of things can occur. I was heading home from work one day and couldn't find my car keys anywhere. Panicked, I headed for the car hoping they weren't locked inside. In the parking garage I discovered the keys in the ignition, with the car running—all day. That's a brain blackout—if you've been there, you know what I mean.

Having a little time to spare before my meeting with Kim and Lisa, I found a chair in the baggage claim area. I sat there and considered my options. I wanted to cry, but I knew that wouldn't do me any good. First I prayed, "Okay, Lord, you've brought me this far, now what? How am I going to get from here to the restaurant?"

I considered just going up to a stranger and asking for a ride. I remember thinking, "People are nicer in the South. I bet someone will take me where I need to go." Then I thought, "Just my luck, I'd end up in a car with an axe murderer, but hey, my troubles would be over!" I thought of heading out to the taxi stand and trying to share a ride with someone, but I didn't know what part of Nashville I was heading to. I didn't have an address, only the name of the restaurant. (Obviously I was not myself—hardly functioning.) Neither of those ideas proved winners, so I just sat there and prayed, "Lord, you know I need a ride. Please send someone."

I knew a bunch of people in Nashville. For ten years I had produced a live concert series for Moody Radio called the Friday Sing. I thought of all the people I knew who could potentially show up at the airport. Michael Card, Buddy Greene, Avalon, Selah, and the list went on. My eyes were on the lookout. I felt certain that God would bring someone along. So I sat, and I sat, and I sat, and I finally said, "This is crazy. God doesn't work like this. What am I thinking?" It was 10:00 a.m. on a Monday and the airport was like a ghost town.

From where I was sitting in baggage claim, I could see the bottom half of the down escalator. Every once in a while someone would come down. I'd see feet, then legs, then a torso, then a head. "Nope, don't know her. Never seen him before. Here comes another one." It felt like I sat there watching, waiting, forever, though it was probably all of twenty minutes, all the while seeing feet, legs, body, and head, not seeing anyone familiar. I was just about to get up and try something else, don't ask me what, when another person riding the escalator came into view. Feet, legs, body, head: "Hey, wait a minute! That's Steve Green."

To some, Steve was like a rock star, but because of my job producing concerts, he was just a friend. I had known Steve for years. I jumped up off my seat and bounded toward him, my eyes welling with tears. Then he saw me and looked surprised. "Anita, what are you doing here?"

As nonchalantly as I could, I said, "Looking for a ride."

Steve said, "Come on. Marijean is waiting for me at the curb. Where are you going?"

If the story wasn't fantastic enough, I had been thinking of the list of people I could potentially see at the Nashville airport, but you've got to know this: Steve Green wasn't on the list. I knew that Steve always rode on his bus. He rarely flew, and he always rolled back into town late Saturday night so he and his ministry staff could be with their families in church Sunday morning. As we walked to the car, I asked, "So what are you doing in the airport on a Monday morning?"

He said, "We took a very rare Sunday concert, and I decided to fly back because it was a really long trip and I had some frequent flyer miles."

My heart nearly exploded with gratitude—to Steve, yes, but mostly to God. "God, did you arrange this for me?" I knew he had. He knew I needed affirmation of his love and care. Have you ever seen God work like that? It can take your breath away.

Steve and Marijean dropped me off at the restaurant where I was to meet Kim and Lisa. God directed every second of that transformational day, including the conversation I had with Steve and Marijean Green on the way to the Green Hills Grill.

Kim talked out of the pain of her own failed marriage, and Lisa shared a wealth of wisdom from her years in women's ministry. They listened; they guided; they challenged some of my misconceptions; they encouraged me in my faith. My emotional tank was full at the end of that divine appointment of a day. Before taking me to the airport, Lisa dropped Kim off at her home. Kim asked us to hold on a minute—she had something she wanted to give me. She ran inside and came out and handed me a sealed card. "Oh, thank you," I said as I slipped it into my still-coinless bag.

I didn't look at the card until I had gone through security. Sitting at the Southwest gate, waiting to board, reflecting on the day, I pulled it out and opened it. Something fell on my lap, but before I looked at that, I read Kim's quickly scrawled note: "God really impressed on my heart that I should give you this. I don't know if you have a need, but God knows." In my lap sat a folded check. "Oh, wasn't that thoughtful," I thought. And then I opened it and read the amount: $2,000. That's two thousand dollars! I sat there and wept. People all around the gate seating area stared at me, but I couldn't help it. I sat there and cried like a baby—overwhelmed by the faithfulness of God.

I had never mentioned finances that day with Kim and Lisa, and I didn't even tell them I couldn't afford the ride from the airport to the restaurant. I only mentioned that I'd run into Steve and that he and Marijean had given me a ride.

JOURNALING THE EXAMEN

As a single parent, I honed the spiritual discipline of journaling. On *Midday Connection* you hear Melinda and me talk often about journaling. We believe it is a spiritual practice with transformative powers. As you dialogue with God through writing, often important issues come to light.

I began journaling in earnest when I was going through my divorce. I signed up for a class at my church called Growing Your Soul, a nine-month intensive small group experience. We met for an hour and a half weekly and had two group retreats and one solo retreat. Author, speaker, and retreat leader Adele Calhoun was codirector and founder of the Growing Your Soul course, and she was my group leader. Adele was in the process of writing her *Spiritual Disciplines Handbook* the year I was in her group. She tested material on the group often.

One week she taught us the spiritual discipline of the examen. Adele explained, "The examen is a practice for discerning the voice and activity of God within the flow of the day. It is a vehicle that creates deeper awareness of God-given desires in one's life."[1] The practice includes a regular time of coming into the presence of God and asking two questions. There are various wordings of the two possible questions, such as, "What are you most grateful for today? What are you least grateful for today?" or "What was the most life-giving moment you experienced today?" "What was the most life-draining moment of your day?" and so on.

I decided to do this exercise daily with my son, John. As he was just nine at the time, I used this wording: "What was your high point and what was your low point today?" I decided to journal both our responses. I did this for about three and a half months.

To signify that we were coming into the presence of God, each evening at bedtime I lit a large candle and carried it into

John's bedroom. I would then pose the examen questions, and we would both answer them. I bought a journal to record our answers, and I would carry this into John's room too. I didn't trust my memory, so I would record our responses then and there. It is still informative to look back at this journal full of things I am grateful to God for, those things that were going well during this difficult time of life, as well as the life-draining moments. I had many low points that centered on loneliness and John's migraine headaches, but some wonderful high points surrounding times with friends. Relationships developed during those difficult years as a single parent that are still solid and strong today.

It is especially helpful for me to look back and see John's responses during this difficult time and to see how far we have both come. God did not leave us there to languish.

If you want to get started journaling and aren't sure how, try using the spiritual discipline of the examen as an entry point to journaling. You don't have to use a paper journal either. That is my preferred method of journaling, but my friend Gail MacDonald always journals on the computer. I have other friends who journal on scraps of paper and then glue them into a notebook. The method isn't important—just do it!

JOURNALING MY GRATITUDE

I transitioned from journaling the examen questions to noting important experiences and God sightings in another journal. Here's a story from my journal of gratitude.

One of John's and my biggest yearly adventures together was our twenty-four-hour drive to northern Maine for summer vacation. To this day we still love road trips. We couldn't afford to fly when I was a single mom, so I mapped out the best route and we drove two looooong days to get to Littleton, Maine.

One year on the third of July, we drove as far as Binghamton, New York, and spent the night. The next morning we set out nice and early, and had been on the road about thirty minutes when a deer ran out in front of us. *Hold on!* I hit the brakes; the deer hit the left front bumper, catapulted up, and landed in the center of the windshield on the driver's side, shattering it. Thankfully I had slowed down enough that the air bag didn't deploy, or the situation would have been even worse. As we came to a stop, the deer bounced off the windshield and lay on the side of the road for about four seconds before bounding away.

"John, are you okay?" I asked.

"Yeah, but what just happened?"

"We just got hit by a deer."

"Yikes, are you okay, Mom?" John had been engrossed in a handheld video game in the backseat and missed most of what happened. I turned off the ignition and we got out of the car to assess the damage.

We wouldn't be driving to Maine today. The left front quarter panel was badly damaged and needed replacing. The hood was dented, and of course the front windshield was barely holding together. Little pieces of glass littered the driver's side dashboard and seat. It was my first accident as a licensed driver. I'd had one accident when I had my learner's permit and was driving on a one-lane road in northern Maine coming to the top of a blind hill. It was so long ago, and my dad took care of everything. It was up to me now. What to do? We had a cell phone, but wouldn't you know we were in a dead zone.

Here I was, alone with my child, standing on the side of the road, in the middle of nowhere, on the Fourth of July. Surely we were stuck here until the holiday weekend was over. All I could see were dollar signs. Money that I didn't have. It was a defining moment for me. Would I panic or would I relax, think, be an adult, and take charge?

John and I prayed together then—and several times at crucial junctures later in the day. I realized I needed to get to a place where my cell phone would work so I could call AAA. Thankfully I'd paid for the deluxe plan that allows for free towing up to one hundred miles. John and I got back in the car, and by sticking my head out the window I managed to drive up the road to a turnaround. There I headed back toward an exit I had passed on the other side of the expressway. I finally got a signal for my cell and called AAA. I was on hold a long time while they tried to find someplace, anyplace, that was open on the holiday.

God provided a kind man who owned a small garage. He towed us and offered to fix our car, though he said it would take three or four days to get the parts (it was, after all, a holiday weekend) and complete the repairs. John and I stared at each other. "There goes our vacation." We didn't plan on spending it in Afton, New York. We prayed for wisdom.

When the garage owner offered to drive us thirty miles to the Binghamton airport—"After all, you have a hundred miles of free towing under your plan, so that covers the extra thirty miles"—so we could rent a car, we effusively thanked him. And praised God. He said that he and his wife had to be over in Binghamton near the end of the next week, and they'd leave my repaired car in the airport parking lot for me to pick up when I returned the rental car on my way back through to Chicago. "I'll bill your insurance company for the work and that should take care of everything." By 2:00 p.m. we were back on the road headed for points north. We reached Grandma and Grandpa's at 2:00 a.m., tired and emotionally tattered. I don't know when I had ever been so happy to be "back home."

COMMUNITY SUPPORT

I believe that single moms and their children are part of the "orphans and widows" mentioned in James 1:27: "Religion that God our Father accepts as pure and faultless is this: to look after orphans and widows in their distress."

The phrase "widows and orphans" appears throughout the Old Testament. Consider Exodus 22:22–23: "Do not take advantage of a widow or an orphan. If you do and they cry out to me, I will certainly hear their cry." Nancy Fuchs-Kreimer notes that "widows and orphans frequently represent all economically vulnerable people, especially in passages in Deuteronomy that set up a crude system of redistributive justice for a primarily agrarian society."[2] She's referring to gleaning, as described in Deuteronomy 24:19: "When you are harvesting in your field and you overlook a sheaf, do not go back to get it. Leave it for the alien, the fatherless and the widow, so that the LORD your God may bless you in all the work of your hands."

Surviving is what most single moms are trying to do or wondering how to do better. As a single mother, I knew if I didn't build some kind of support system, I'd be toast.

I felt it was important to stay active and connected in the life of my church. I got involved singing on a worship team for the contemporary service, and that's where I met a woman named Sandy. Sandy had a son John's same age. Having same-age boys and our mutual love for music created an immediate bond. If you're struggling as a single woman, I suggest you also connect with your current church—or a new church if change is important. If you can take your child to church with you and then go to an adult Sunday school class when your child is in Sunday school, you'll have the opportunity to build a relational network for yourself.

A *Midday Connection* listener asked, "How do I go about

finding my son a mentor?" I suggest you start at your church. You'll need to build your own network of friends first, but often those relationships will bring with them what you need for your child. Other options, depending on where you live and the age of your child, might be Boys and Girls Clubs or Boy Scouts and Girl Scouts. Involve them in youth group if they are of middle school or high school age. That can be a critical time in the life of your child.

Another listener keenly commented, "For those who aren't single parents, please reach out to the single parents and their children who are around you. You might even want to think about sort of making them a part of your family—single parent included."

That's exactly what happened for me. I was blessed to have two families who stepped up big-time in my life. My friend Sandy and my friend Faith regularly invited John and me over for holidays and family meals. Faith's husband, Ray, would often cook and invite John to help him in the kitchen. To this day John still loves to help out whenever I'm cooking. Whatever Ray was doing with his own kids, he would include John.

As we shared our stories, Sandy realized I was a single mom and started inviting John and me over for dinners often on Sunday nights. The boys would play, and Sandy and I would have more time to talk and get to know each other. Sandy's husband, John, would often corral the boys to help with some project either in the yard or in the basement depending on the time of year. John especially loved these interactions with "Mr. Towers." I became comfortable enough that often John and I would just drop by. I come from northern Maine, which is a culture where dropping in on someone is a welcome thing. Not everyone feels that way, but the Towerses did, and it meant so much to know I could drop by anytime and let my hair down and John had a friend to play with too.

I remember leaving Sandy's house one Sunday evening. This was when John was eight or nine years old. We got in the car and John said, "Can't I just stay here? I want to live with the Towerses." I know some moms might have been hurt by that statement, and I admit that I felt a twinge of pain, sensing that what I could offer would never measure up to the ideal. And yet I was so grateful for this family that had become family to us. They truly were "Jesus" to us.

For several years Faith's family lived kitty-corner to us, and John would often go there after school before I came home from work. We were a part of many of their family events, even after we moved away. John still goes back to the old neighborhood to go trick-or-treating with the Lee kids. It's a tradition. They are like siblings to him. When the oldest Lee headed to college this past year, she invited John to come with her sister and brother to "sibling weekend."

I was thankful that he could see the body of Christ at work as these Christian families reached out to us. How much of that did he grasp as an eight-year-old? Plenty.

TAKE CHARGE

I also learned during the single-mom years how to be more of an adult and take responsibility for my needs. Part of growing up and being an adult is being able to state your needs to the people in your life and taking charge and stepping up to the plate to fix your own problems. Many single moms have trouble asking for help. Actually, most of us have trouble asking for help. As a single mom, take a risk: try to state your needs to a friend. No one can read your mind, and as much as the church should be proactive in helping, that's not always the case. I learned to ask Faith if John could come over and play so I could run errands, or when I needed to stay late at work. If she couldn't do it, she would tell me. If we don't learn how to make our needs known, our needs often will go unmet, and we become frustrated and exhausted. It takes a certain kind of energy on the front end just to ask, but you'll be surprised how people want to help if given the opportunity. God knows your needs and he wants to provide for you. Be bold in prayer and in action.

As I took charge of my life, I learned to take my car to the mechanic for regular oil changes. I learned what to do and whom to call when I had a flooded basement and when my water pipes froze up in the winter. I knew no one else was responsible except me. Taking charge when there is a problem can be a confidence booster to a single mom. It doesn't mean you can't ask for help and take others up on their willing service, but you have to be the initiator.

INSIGHT FROM LISTENERS

I've been encouraged by advice submitted by *Midday* listeners in response to programs about single parenting. One single mother succinctly identified her three single-parent roles as initiator, enforcer, and regulator. She is quick to initiate conversation, reconciliation, and restoration when needed. As the enforcer, she is not afraid to hold the line and stand by the boundaries she's set up. And as the regulator of all things, she watches over food and snack consumption, health issues, media use, and schedules.

One twenty-six-year-old daughter who seems to have thrived in a single-parent home praised her mother for being honest about life and about her father "without being negative." This can be one of the hardest issues for a single mom. Whether you are single due to divorce or never having married, the temptation is there to say negative things about "Dad."

In my county in Illinois, a parenting class is required if you go through a divorce. I begrudgingly went assuming I would not learn anything new. God spoke to my heart during that class; who would have thought? One of the major points made, or at least the major point I heard, was the importance of talking positively to your child about your ex-spouse, or at least not negatively. If there are illegal behaviors or inappropriate actions taking place, those must be confronted, but your ex-spouse is part of your child. To say bad things about the other parent is, in essence, to say bad things about your child.

The twenty-six-year-old daughter also praised her mother for providing spiritual guidance. "She introduced us to God through church and life in general. My mother showed me who and what God could be in my life." I clung to her words as I too worked to make God real to my young son.

STAND FIRM

As John moved into the middle school years, life got a little more challenging. No surprise there. The middle school youth group, COW (Cloud of Witnesses), met on Wednesday nights. I knew the value of community and wanted him to experience it. I wanted to make sure he got plugged in at church, but he dug in his heels and didn't want to go. He hated going, dreaded going, and one of the hardest things I had to do during the single-mom years was to push him and make him go to COW. He would voice his concerns and dislikes and I would talk to Andy, the middle school youth director.

The complaints continued for a year and a half. Finally one night after I picked him up, he said, "Mom, it was awesome tonight. Some kids told their story and then asked if anyone else wanted to tell their story and kids just got up and started sharing, and I got up and told my story. It was amazing!"

I silently praised God as John told me how great his night had been. All the months and months of standing firm had paid off. Holding the line like that is one of the toughest jobs of a single parent. There is no backup, and most single moms are moments away from exhaustion all the time.

We were riding in the car one evening after I'd picked John up from the high school youth group (Koinonia), when he said to me, "Mom, thanks for making me go to COW all those nights when I didn't want to go. I know I made it really hard on you, but I wouldn't be who I am today if you hadn't made me go. I love Koinonia."

I hope that story encourages you to persevere. When our children push back and it takes all we have to stand our ground—and be initiator, enforcer, and regulator—keep standing firm. It will pay dividends down the road. There are days it doesn't seem like it, but children are a treasure from the Lord.

DISCUSSION QUESTIONS

1. If you are a single mom, what has been the most difficult aspect of single parenting?

2. What does the support network around you look like? Of whom is it comprised?

3. When was a time you saw God show up in an unmistakable way for you and your children?

4. Has the church been a safe place where you've been able to build community? Why or why not?

5. Have you ever invited a single mom and her children over for a meal or worked to develop a relationship with them? What was that experience like?

6. How can you or your church help to support single moms?

chapter seven

BLESS THE BROKEN ROAD

What Women Tell Me:

I came to know Christ a month after my divorce and began going through divorce recovery at a large local church and found healing. Seventeen years later now, I am still single (now fifty), still waiting for God's Best.

I have a friend who has been through a divorce recently, and I have been surprised by how quickly she has sought to get back into a relationship—even going about it in ways that seem desperate. I can't help but think that she is way too focused on remarrying, especially when she has two really out-of-control young children.

• • •

I CAN REMEMBER THE BUTTERFLIES IN my stomach as if it were yesterday. I got up that morning, knowing this was the day I would take off my wedding ring. I'd thought about doing it many times prior, but something kept me from going that far. I twirled it around and around on my finger. Part of me wanted to pull it off and throw it as far as I could. Another part of me didn't want to face what taking it off really meant. I finally did take it off. In a matter-of-fact way, I put it in a small section of my jewelry armoire never to be worn again.

I took the day off work knowing I'd have nothing left in my tank after the pronouncement. Several friends had asked if I wanted them to accompany me, but I knew this was something I needed to do alone. I drove to the courthouse thinking, "How did it come to this?" Not that I hadn't already asked that question a hundred times. Today was the day. Despite counseling and confession, prayer and pleading, my marriage had ended. It was the end of a dream and the beginning of a walk down a very broken road. I was sad, sick to my stomach, afraid, tired, and yet somehow happy to be able to move forward. The tears had all been cried.

I entered the courthouse stoically. I sat with my attorney, signed a stack of papers, and awkwardly waited for my name to be called. I halfway smiled at the thought that this might be the last legal bill I would receive. The breakup of a marriage is expensive on many levels, the least of which is financial. The judge called my name and pronounced my marriage officially over with the crack of his gavel.

ME, THE PHARISEE

For too many years I was a person lacking in grace and quick to point my finger in judgment. I spent the greater part of my life with a critical spirit, actively pointing out the imperfections and sins in others. I was not very different from the Pharisees in Jesus' day. Because I wanted to make sure everything looked good on the outside, getting divorced didn't fit the picture very well. It certainly didn't fit the neat, tidy, evangelical picture I'd painted for my life and that I believed others around me had painted as well.

Matthew 23 described me, but I didn't see it until my life started to unravel. I was a Pharisee but totally blind to it. I looked down on the Pharisees and couldn't believe they could be so focused on only externals. I would read Matthew 23:25–28 and believe this description was the farthest thing from me.

> *"Woe to you, teachers of the law and Pharisees, you hypocrites! You clean the outside of the cup and dish, but inside they are full of greed and self-indulgence. Blind Pharisee! First clean the inside of the cup and dish, and then the outside also will be clean.*
>
> *"Woe to you, teachers of the law and Pharisees, you hypocrites! You are like whitewashed tombs, which look beautiful on the outside but on the inside are full of dead men's bones and everything unclean. In the same way, on the outside you appear to people as righteous but on the inside you are full of hypocrisy and wickedness."*

Jesus' words in Matthew 23 are his last public message. Warren Wiersbe says, "It is a scathing denunciation of false religion that paraded under the guise of truth. Some of the common people no doubt were shocked at His words, for they considered the Pharisees to be righteous."[1] That was my problem. I considered myself to be righteous. Jesus said, "But do not do what [the Pharisees] do, for they do not practice what they preach. They tie up heavy, cumbersome loads and put them on other people's shoulders, but they themselves are not willing to lift a finger to move them. Everything they do is done for people to see" (Matthew 23:3–5 TNIV). I looked good on the outside, but I was dying on the inside. In my real life, I had just been hit by hurricane-force winds and didn't know what to do about it.

Even while going through the lengthy legal proceedings leading up to my divorce, I was comforted by the fact that as long as the process was still happening, I couldn't be called a divorced woman. One woman said, "I'd been divorced for ten years; was I going to have to wear the 'D' forever?" I'd been at more than one gathering and overheard, "You know, she's divorced. I don't know what happened, but they say . . ." Or "She used to come to church here, but, you know, she's divorced. We're better off without her kind here." Those were the lingering whispers swirling around my mind. What really hurt was realizing that although I hadn't said those same things, I'd thought them. I was a Pharisee.

How did I turn into a Pharisee? I mean, I was a preacher's kid. Here are some of the messages I received as a preacher's kid: "You'd better behave! What will people think? You've got to set a good example. You're not just anybody's daughter; you're the preacher's daughter. Isn't she a lovely little lady, so dainty and feminine? She is dressed so beautifully for church, not a hair out of place." Comments like these came over and over from parents, grandparents, deacons' wives, and Sunday school teachers. I can't blame them for the life I chose to live, but like a "good girl," I lived what I was told. I learned that I was rewarded for good behavior and outward appearance.

I fell comfortably into my conservative evangelical culture that told me not to drink or dance or smoke or chew. And just to play it safe, I added going to movies and using playing cards as a couple of additional don'ts. And I wouldn't be caught rubbing shoulders with anyone engaging in questionable activities. I guess I glossed over Mark 2:15 – 17.

While Jesus was having dinner at Levi's house, many tax collectors and "sinners" were eating with him and his disciples, for there were many who followed him. When the teachers of the law who were Pharisees saw him eating with the "sinners" and tax collectors, they asked his disciples: "Why does he eat with tax collectors and 'sinners'?"

On hearing this, Jesus said to them, "It is not the healthy who need a doctor, but the sick. I have not come to call the righteous, but sinners."

The day I went into my boss's office to tell him my husband and I were in the midst of a marriage crisis and were separating was a difficult day, but nothing like the day I had to tell him my marriage was over. I couldn't use the "D" word. In fact, it was a couple of years before I could even say the word *divorce*. Divorce was something that happened to other people, people who weren't as godly as I was. What would people think? The real question was, what would people think of *me*?

I was afraid of losing my job, and I was afraid that every Christian who passed me was thinking, "Are there biblical grounds for her divorce? Whose fault was it? Did she do everything possible to save her marriage?" I knew their thoughts, because those had been my thoughts. I used to sit in judgment of people like me. "Can't they get their act together?" I'd think when I heard a couple was having marital problems. Or "Didn't they say before God and everyone else 'till death do us part'?" Or "They must not really be Christians, or they wouldn't let this happen." I didn't have a template to work with when *I* was the one going through a divorce. The snide, critical thoughts didn't work anymore. This was my life, my new shattered reality.

For the first time in my life, I saw myself as a sinner in need of a Savior. I don't mean I wasn't a Christian. I had begun my faith journey as a seven-year-old, but sometimes it's hard to grasp your need for salvation when you're a child. I always knew in my head I was a sinner saved by grace, but I had never really understood what it meant to be a sinner. And I certainly had never really held an understanding of God's grace. I'd never needed that understanding before.

Going through a divorce rocked my world and showed me the volume of pride filling my heart. "How could I be letting the cause of Christ down like this?" As if it all depended on me! When I saw the magnitude of my pride, it was crushing. There were days when I could hardly hold my emotions at bay. I would put my son to bed at night and let the torrents flow. I had to repent of the years I sat in judgment of others, the years I considered myself righteous all on my own, not because of what Christ had done.

Then I turned a corner. I had never showed much emotion, so letting tears flow was a new experience for me. I don't remember the exact day, but I saw a shift in the reason for my tears. Instead of tears of repentance, they turned to tears of gratefulness to God for his amazing grace. I not only saw the depths of my sin, but believed the forgiveness I'd been given and began splashing in the puddles of God's grace that I started seeing everywhere. I told a friend, "It feels so good to feel, to express emotion and not care what anyone thinks." (As you can see, there was a lot of "caring what people thought" — that's one of the by-products of pride.)

I remember a faculty member stopping me one day as I was leaving campus for home. "Anita, I've been catching your program more frequently, and I don't know if something has happened in your life, but you are much more authentic these days. I just want to encourage you to keep on the same track."

"Yeah, I've experienced some things lately that God has used to change me. Thanks for the encouragement." I walked on toward my car with tears flowing again in thankfulness of God's ongoing grace in my life. "I am changing, I have changed. Thank you, God!"

GOD'S TENDERNESS

Let's go back to Matthew 23. After Jesus finishes delivering the seven woes to the teachers of the Law and the Pharisees, he talks about Jerusalem and what Israel was bringing upon herself. And in a tender tone he says, "How often I have longed to gather your children together, as a hen gathers her chicks under her wings, but you were not willing" (v. 37). Matthew Henry says, "A hen gathering her chickens under her wings is an apt emblem of the Saviour's tender love to those who trust in him, and his faithful care of them. He calls sinners to take refuge under his tender protection, keeps them safe, and nourishes them to eternal life."[2]

I was a long way down the road before I saw the reality of my sin and the truth of God's grace if I would just entrust myself to his care. I've never been a fan of the melody, but in the past ten years the lyrics of the hymn "Jesus, Thy Blood and Righteousness" have often run through my head, especially the first line of the song: "Jesus, thy blood and righteousness my beauty are, my glorious dress."

Even through the Old English verbiage, I love the thought that I am dressed in Christ's blood, in his righteousness. My beauty has nothing to do with me, but everything to do with him. That takes all the pressure off.

As I started coming out on the other side of my pride, casting myself on the mercy of Christ, I realized I had an opportunity to speak truth about God's grace into the hearts of those listening to *Midday Connection*, and to those with whom I worked and attended church. As one example, just after my divorce was final, there was a knock on my office door.

"Anita, can I talk to you about something personal?"

"Sure," I said. I anticipated an informal counseling session. The conversation was more complicated than I'd expected.

"I've never known anyone who's been divorced. I know you're still working here, so it must be okay, but is it really okay?"

I hadn't seen it coming. I took a deep breath and dove into the deep end of the pool. "I've learned a lot over the past few years, not the least of which is how broken I am. I've always said we live in a broken world but didn't see myself as one of the broken. I am. Now I swim in the pool of God's grace, but it took me a long time to do more than just dip my toe into that water. I certainly don't believe that God's best plans center on divorce, but I've learned that God will use whatever it takes to draw us closer to himself. I believe he cares more about the individual than he does the institution of marriage. People might try to sideline me, but God never will. With all the pain I experienced and will experience as I go forward raising John jointly with his dad, I wouldn't go back to the way life was. I certainly didn't welcome this crisis, but I wouldn't trade it for anything for the work God did in my heart. Does that answer your question?"

That was the end of the conversation. I offered to answer any further questions anytime. No one else came asking, though some people pulled away. Now, more than ten years later, some of those relationships are repaired, but not all.

It's hard enough going through a divorce, but it's doubly difficult going through one in the midst of a conservative culture. The struggle is that we put the Word of God in one hand and compassion in the other, and the two don't always meet. Grace and truth go hand in hand in Scripture. Psalm 85:10 reads, "Mercy and truth are met together; righteousness and peace have kissed each other" (KJV). When mercy and truth meet, it usually means there's a mess to clean up. Often it's easier to sit in judgment.

In one of my favorite devotionals, *The Miraculous Journey*, Mary Bullis talks about Jesus being the light in a mucky world. *Mucky*, that's my kind of word. "Relationship is difficult in our darkened world. We live in a mucky place: full of lies, divorce, anger, abuse and pride. We've all had our share of getting beaten up by living in relationship, and we've all done our share of not respecting those around us.... Christ enters into the muck to live with us, to be in relation with us. He's the only thing we can see that is *full of grace*.... He's light for living with our families, grace for sticking at it with neighbors, balm for our relational hurts."[3]

DIVORCE RECOVERY

I've gone to church all my life, but I had never heard of "divorce recovery" until I was in the throes of going through my divorce. When I discovered it I thought, "Why don't most churches have something like this? Hmm. I guess it can be hard to have a divorce recovery program if you don't believe divorce is happening in your church." While that may be a harsh statement, I think the point is valid. Acknowledging that something is happening and planning classes to help those who are going through the pain of divorce doesn't mean that you condone divorce. Divorce *does happen* for all the right and all the wrong reasons. But if, as the church, we aren't poised to help people pick up the pieces, we have ceased to be a hospital for sinners and have become solely a school for soldiers. I believe we can be both, and I especially believe that the soldiers should not be shooting the wounded but instead carrying them on stretchers toward the hospital.

Just before my divorce was final, I started going to divorce recovery. I confess that pride was still an issue; instead of attending the classes with everyone else, I went for one-on-one sessions to the instructor's office. I didn't want people to see me, Anita Lustrea, the host of *Midday Connection*, going to divorce recovery classes. "They might think I am going through a divorce!" Graciously, the pastor of single adults at my church, Andy Morgan, invited me to meet with him to go through the material.

Here's another confession. I didn't think I would learn anything I didn't already know. I hosted a talk show that regularly dealt with divorce, remarriage, and abuse issues; what could I possibly learn? Did I mention I still struggled with pride? God gently showed me a better way as I started reading books and going through a specific workbook and watching videos on divorce recovery. As Jim Smoke, known for his ministry to singles and his divorce recovery seminars, says, "You can go through it ... or grow through it." God helped me to grow through it.

When Andy Morgan left my church, Mike Murphy filled the role of pastor of single adults. Mike said, "One of the questions we ask in Divorce Recovery is, "Regardless of what the end of your marriage looked like, or why it ended, why do you think someone would not choose to spend the rest of their life with you?" Talk about a question that causes soul-searching! It is important to take a look at how you contributed to the dissolution of the marriage. Not for the sake of beating yourself up, but for the sake of the healing that needs to take place in your life. Even if initially there is a presenting issue from your spouse that caused the breakup of the marriage, it is important to look at your contributions. As long as you keep pointing the finger, or standing in a defensive posture, you can't see how you contributed to the problem. It goes back to Matthew 7:2–4 (TNIV):

*"For in the same way you judge others, you will be judged,
and with the measure you use, it will be measured to you.*
*"Why do you look at the speck of sawdust in someone
else's eye and pay no attention to the plank in your own eye?
How can you say, 'Let me take the speck out of your eye,'
when all the time there is a plank in your own eye?"*

Unfortunately, in many conservative evangelical circles, people want to take sides. They feel they need to take sides. There has to be a right party and a wrong party. For a couple of years, I too viewed myself as in the "right." I feared for a long time that if I owned my part, I'd be thrown out of the church as I knew it. Finally, however, I started looking at how I contributed to my failed marriage.

I don't know anyone who stands at the altar secretly hoping that what they're entering into will end in divorce. We all want happily ever after. And yet, statistically, only a few manage "happy," a significant number grit their teeth and persevere, and far too many marriages fall apart. It's a mess. The website www.divorcerate.org keeps up with the current stats on divorce. The media touts that 50 percent of marriages end in divorce; the reality in the United States is a little under that. Approximately 45 percent of first marriages end in divorce. More startling are the stats for second and third marriages: 60 to 65 percent of second marriages and around 73 percent of third marriages end in divorce. The Barna Research Group reports that the divorce rate for evangelical Christians is higher than the national average and higher than other faith groups.[4]

More often than hearing from listeners in the midst of divorce, I hear from those who don't know what to do because a divorced family is attending church. Or they don't know how to even open up a conversation. One listener said both of the divorced parties still attended church, the husband even showing up once with a new girlfriend. "I find it odd that everyone seems okay with this. In my family divorce happened a lot, but my father moved us away from the family so we didn't have to rub shoulders with them." Many of us in the church don't know how to step into the mess alongside others. What would Jesus do? Have a conversation? Possibly ask questions? Maybe even confront? What we do know is Jesus wouldn't back away and do nothing. He is a welcoming presence filled with love and compassion even when addressing those who are in sin.

Another recurring email topic has to do with supporting a woman going through a divorce. "My sister, who is just divorced, is trying to be strong. What can I do to help her?" Empathy is the number one need of hurting people. Listen and love. Practically, ask if you can watch the kids while this sister heads to the grocery store or enjoys an evening out with a girlfriend. Think of the things in your own life that are made easier because you have an intact marriage; that will help you think of other ways to step in and help.

THE SAMARITAN WOMAN

She comes to the well at noontime, in the heat of the day. All the other women come for water in the cooler hours of the morning. I surmise she is trying to escape the prying eyes, the gossipy whispering tongues. She is surprised by the stranger at the well. Even more surprised at this Rabbi asking her, "Will you give me a drink?"

Historically we know the Samaritans were despised by the Jews. Jesus "had to" go through Samaria, the text says, even though most Jewish travelers avoided this land and people. It appears Jesus had an appointment with this woman, who would lead virtually her entire village to Jesus. And through her he affirms all of us who feel sidelined due to sin, shame, false accusations, and less-than-perfect pedigree.

Growing up I always got the impression that the woman at the well was slutty, going from man to man to man. But as I read different commentaries and thought about what the text doesn't say, using my sacred imagination, I began to see that five marriages didn't mean she'd been divorced five times. She could have been widowed two or three times. She probably was divorced and abandoned more than once, as it was very easy for a man to divorce his wife and leave her destitute in Jesus' day. She, I'm sure, looked for another husband each time to have protection and provision for her children and herself if she was a mother. A single woman was not held in high regard in that culture and had little means of surviving financially. In her current relationship she may have been thinking, "If I'm living with him and not married, he can't divorce me. I won't have to go through the pain and humiliation of that again."

This story is important on so many levels. Jesus' treatment of women is highlighted, and so are his treatment of a marginalized race and his willingness to reach out beyond the Jewish people to give salvation. The point I want to camp on is that people may try to sideline you if you've gone through a divorce, but Jesus never will. In their book *Jesus, Lover of a Woman's Soul*, Erwin and Rebecca Lutzer say:

> Might it also be that Jesus used the woman at the well to break down the bias that men had toward women? To prove that the time had come for the double standard to end? That God delights in using women to share His message? And that His message is for everyone, including those whose lives have been marred by a history of

marital failure? ... Jesus saw women not just as souls worth saving but as individuals whose ministry was of great benefit to the Kingdom. The Samaritan woman is a reminder that we don't have to have a perfect record to be used by God in great ways.[5]

Divorce can be the end of your story, or it can be a beautiful beginning as you realize you are on the threshold of a new calling, of being used by God in new ways. As Jan Richardson put it so eloquently: "We may find ourselves at a threshold by choice or by circumstance, arriving by our own design or landing there by events seemingly beyond our control. Whether or not it seems sacred at first, a threshold can become a holy place of new beginnings as we tend it, wait within it, and discern the path beyond."[6]

JESUS' QUESTION TO BARTIMAEUS

Post divorce, if you had told me I'd be remarried someday, I would have laughed in your face. After going through a painful divorce and having a young child at home, albeit only one, I had no desire to bring another complication, as I saw it, into my life. I had thought through the biblical passages on divorce and remarriage and believed biblically I could remarry, but I also felt content as a single woman. A truer statement is I didn't have time to think beyond the day-to-day living of being a single mom to a young child. God, however, had other ideas. It seems he often has other ideas.

At church I had enrolled with eight other people in a nine-month course called Growing Your Soul. With weekly meetings and a lengthy reading list plus two required group retreats and one required solo retreat, I knew I'd get to know my group members well, and I'd grow my soul too. I really looked forward to the group sessions, led by author and speaker Adele Calhoun. This loving community helped walk with me over the broken road of divorce. About four months into the group process, we met on a Saturday for a half-day retreat. Again, I anticipated this gathering and God's word for me.

Adele opened our day with one of my favorite New Testament stories, the story of blind Bartimaeus in Mark 10. If you recall the story, Bartimaeus was a beggar sitting by the roadside when he heard that Jesus was passing by. He didn't care who was around. He started shouting at the top of his lungs, "Jesus, Son of David, have mercy on me!" Everyone around him was trying to shush him. But he kept on. Finally Jesus stopped and said, "Tell him to come here." When Jesus and Bartimaeus were face-to-face, Jesus asked the all-important question, "What do you want me to do for you?" As you might expect, Bartimaeus said, "I want to see!"

Jumping off from this story, Adele asked us to take our Bibles and journals and a handout she had prepared and scatter to the far corners of the house. "Spend a couple of hours with this story," she said. "What is it saying to you? What is Jesus saying to you, and what do you want him to do for you? What is the deepest desire of your heart?" With Bible and journal in hand, I went off to talk to God.

After a quick prayer, asking God to reveal some deep desire, I thought, "I don't know myself very well, because I have no idea what the deepest desire of my heart is." Of course Adele knew we all needed some serious time alone with God on this one.

First I read through the story again, reminding myself of the Scottish reformers who recommended engaging our sacred imagination while reading Scripture. I pictured Jesus standing in front of me as I begged by the side of the road. Then I sensed Jesus asking me, "Anita, what do you want me to do for you?"

I had no idea. I couldn't answer his question. I paused to pray. What was so deep inside that I couldn't access it? And why was it so deep? Had I buried something that I didn't want even God to reach?

For a long time I just sat in my chair drawing a total blank. We were meeting in Adele's home. I'd chosen a little nook with a desk and no window, which is what I needed that day. I couldn't do with the distractions of looking outside. A little worry niggled, "What if I go back to the group when time's up and I have nothing to say, nothing to show for my two hours with God?"

Once I dismissed that and determined this wasn't an exercise in productivity, or success versus failure, I relaxed. That's when God started to move. At first it was just a seed thought. "Love again." This felt right because I wondered if I could love anyone well again. Then I sensed God speaking to me more deeply. "Be loved again." Oh no. I knew what that meant. God meant for me to open up my heart. When that thought fully formed in me, I dissolved into a puddle of tears. Adele walked around the house to let us know we had about five more minutes. I knew I couldn't get myself back together in five, so I went to the kitchen and made a cup of tea and was the last to rejoin the group in the living room.

I regained my composure while others shared their insights with the group. But when my turn came to speak, I barely got a word out when I lost it again. I pride myself on being an emotionally even-keeled woman. I guess *pride* is the operative word there. Basically, I never wanted anyone to see me express emotion, which was its own problem. One of those family-of-origin gifts, if you know what I mean. Thankfully, it's a gift I've thrown away. All pride went out the window as I struggled to tell the group what God had unveiled to me as my deepest heart's desire: to remarry. But the desire went deeper: to experience marriage in a right way, a whole way, a healthy way, like I had never experienced it before.

There was so much fear surrounding the desire that only God could have pried it loose. Like many who've been through a traumatic divorce, I confronted fear-based questions and statements. Who would want me? I was damaged goods. I had a child. I didn't want to disrupt life for my child. Would I marry someone with children? This would take work. How would I find the right man? What would it take to heal so I could be ready for another relationship someday? This deep desire was overwhelming in scope.

My group members didn't help. Considering the flow of emotion, I was expecting a warm, understanding response. Instead, several of them launched into a strategy to set me up with someone who was single in our congregation. It was one of those highly insensitive moments, yet none of them saw it that way. Their intentions were pure — they just wanted to see me realize my deepest desire — but badly timed.

DESIRE REALIZED

I confess that after this desire bubbled up to the surface, I became a bit obsessed with God's plan for me. I was in the middle of going through a divorce recovery program. I knew I needed personal healing for the past, but I had no thought toward the future. As I mentioned earlier, a group program is invaluable as it engages you in addressing issues you wouldn't have thought of, or that you purposely would have avoided. Everyone, no exceptions, who has been through a divorce needs to go through divorce recovery.

As God was working in my heart, little did I know that one of the pastors of my church was in the midst of a very difficult divorce after thirty-one years of marriage. When you hold a job that puts you in the public eye, and you are in ministry, divorce becomes that much more complex. When I heard of his situation, I identified with his pain. The church moved him from the position of family pastor to pastor of single adults. Eventually I went to see him to ask if he wanted to talk, or to make sure he had supportive people around him to help him work through his public divorce. At the close of our time together, I opened the door for him to be a guest on *Midday Connection* to talk about ministry to singles after he had been in that position awhile.

Months later I invited Mike to be a guest on *Midday Connection*, and then to have lunch afterward. The food was terrible, but the conversation was great. We talked through all the intricacies of going through a public divorce while engaging in ministry. We understood each other on many levels because of that. We talked about what it's like to be in such pain but still carry on in ministry like you're perfectly fine and nothing is wrong. I talked about being a mom to a young son and barely having the energy to meet his needs after a long workday. To have someone who understood was a true gift.

Mike asked me what I did on nights when John was with his dad. I told him, "I often eat at Portillo's. It gives me a break from my own cooking, and I take a book and read because it's the one night I don't have to punch a clock. I run errands and grocery shop after that."

Before we left our lunch, Mike said, "Maybe I can join you sometime when you go to Portillo's." I confess my heart fluttered a tiny bit.

It sounds like I'm telling a love story. I'm really telling two. Sure, I found myself falling in love with Mike Murphy. But the overarching love story was of God's love for me. He loved me enough to allow crisis into my life to move me closer to him, and then he loved me enough to make me dig deep to see the bigger issues and the better things he had planned for me.

Mike and I continued to see each other, and he asked me to share the stage with him to help teach three hundred singles in a fall series about relationships. We spent the whole summer delving into topics of interest for single adults: communication, relationship myths, habits of men, habits of women, even sex, though when we got to that topic we found it a little difficult, so we pulled out our sunglasses (not rose-colored) to engage in that conversation. We spent about seventy hours talking about the important relational issues between men and women, and in the process we found out a lot about each other. As we began to explore what an ongoing relationship between us might look like, some relational guidelines emerged.

RELATIONSHIP RULES

Relationships take time: time to get to know another person, and after a divorce, time to heal. Earlier I mentioned the staggering statistic that approximately 60 percent of second marriages end in divorce, and Mike and I didn't take that figure lightly. We wanted to do everything possible to beat that statistic if we decided to remarry.

Many who have experienced divorce head down the dating path before they've had time to heal. They head into rebound relationships. That's part of why the divorce rate for second marriages is so high. One listener, responding to a *Midday Connection* guest who had proposed reasons why some people date right after the divorce, wrote, "We try to find the person who lets us know we are worthwhile and worth loving, that we have value. Trying to find a Band-Aid to put over the open wound does not work." Sometimes we let our hearts and our hormones rule. I don't care if you're twenty-five or fifty-five; we are created as sexual beings. Mike and I knew we needed to listen to our heads, not our hormones.

Although we felt God was bringing us together, we had learned that it was important to go through all four seasons with someone before getting married. There are issues that come up at holiday times for those who might marry, and the only way to see and experience those issues is to walk through the seasons together. It's also important to see if the person you might marry has experienced the healing he or she needs. You want to see the other person in good times and bad. It takes time to meet family and friends, to worship together, to explore where the other person is spiritually. You want to see how the other person treats others, everyone from family to colleagues to waiters, repairmen, and taxi drivers. You'd be surprised what you can learn by taking time and being observant. Don't let anyone rush you, especially the person you are dating. At one point that was me. When I pressed for marriage, Mike lovingly said, "No, we need to experience all four seasons together, and you'll be thankful we did." He was right.

When we did make the decision to marry again, we understood that the necessary preparation was key. We went to a marriage counselor. Neither of us had proper marriage counseling the first time around. We read a lot of relationship books and took the Prepare-Enrich Inventory, an excellent tool many churches and counselors use to put a mirror up to a couple's relationship, letting them see where their relational strengths and weaknesses are. We wanted to make sure we understood what was happening inside us individually and as a couple, and what God was saying to us as well as what other Christian leaders had to say about healing and remarriage.

Don't shortchange your preparation. One listener who has been remarried for more than five years—with "his and hers" teen children—notes that their marriage is thriving because "we realized how fragile a marriage relationship is and we were willing to look at what part each of us played in the failure of our first marriages." She sees communication as "the key to everything" and feels they've both learned to value "being vulnerable, being humble, and loving each other as God loves us." Let me add that if you are having a difficult time communicating during the marriage preparation time, or if your significant other won't share from his heart and life, his sharing will only decrease after marriage. Pay attention to this important part of communicating.

What do good friends have to say about the person you are interested in? Sometimes we surround ourselves with people who tell us what we want to hear. Mike and I both knew people who would tell us the truth. I remember Mike taking me to a Fourth of July gathering with some of his friends I'd not met. As we walked up to the front door, I said, "This is really important, isn't it?"

Mike said, "Yes," and I felt the weight of his response.

Later he told me, "If these friends didn't see what I was seeing, or saw something in me they didn't like, they'd tell me. Their opinion mattered. If they'd said, 'Ease off,' or 'We don't think this is the right thing,' chances are we wouldn't still be dating." Make sure you spend time with your prospective partner around trusted friends who will speak the truth.

One of the biggest mistakes people make is entering into a second marriage being unequally yoked. I don't just mean marrying someone who doesn't have a relationship with Christ. I also mean marrying someone who isn't on the same page spiritually, someone with no desire to go deeper in faith. Another listener relayed wise counsel received from a counselor who used the image of "a triangle with both of us at the bottom and God at the top. The closer we get to God, the closer we get to each other. This is not to say we had no problems ... but we *always* talk about things and hide nothing ... because it's so vital!" In the best marriages and remarriages, there will be bumps in the road. If you are not on the same spiritual trajectory, you are already in a deficit position.

Something else many couples do not examine is their relational history, not just in marriage, but in all relationships. If you've struggled relationally inside and outside of marriage, you need to take a look at that. A realistic and honest look at your relational history will go a long way in determining whether remarriage is the right step for you.

Another consideration in the decision to remarry is children. I had a young son. Mike's children were grown and on their own. At one point I had determined I would not marry someone who had children, because I thought doing so would turn John's world upside down. But God had made clear what he wanted me to do. Mike never thought he'd remarry anyone with children still at home, but God opened his heart up to me and to John.

SURPRISE WEDDING

Mike and I married in July 2005. It was a Wednesday, and we headed to the usual midweek meeting of the singles group where Mike was pastor. The night was part of a special summer series. Buddy Greene was the special guest performer. Mike opened up the evening to those who had married and no longer attended the singles group and to some others in the church, so the usual three hundred had swelled to five hundred.

At the beginning of the evening, Senior Pastor Dan Meyer announced Mike's and my engagement, to much applause. We had decided to bookend the evening with another surprise.

Buddy's concert ended with the announcement, "After the final song, everyone should head to the garden chapel, because Mike and Anita will be getting married." Our surprise wedding ended the evening, with Buddy's promise to play processional and recessional music (his entertaining version of "Jesu, Joy of Man's Desiring" turning into the William Tell Overture). Because many in attendance had brought cameras to photograph the concert, Mike and I had built-in wedding photographers.

More than five years later, Mike and I are still vigilant in our marriage. We never let the sun go down on our anger (Ephesians 4:26). We believe the best in each other and always give each other the benefit of the doubt. We continue to fill up each other's emotional bank account so when a sizable withdrawal is needed, there is margin. We live in community, not isolation, and both of us have friends who speak the truth in love to us as we do to them. We have an ongoing, growing relationship with Christ that is foundational to everything else. All a result of lessons learned the hard way.

DISCUSSION QUESTIONS

1. What has been your experience dealing with divorce? Has it been personal, going through a failed marriage yourself, or have you known others who have gone through divorce?

2. The Christian community sometimes makes people feel that divorce is the unforgivable sin. What is so threatening about divorce for the average Christian and church?

3. How does your church support those who are divorced? Is there something it could do better?

4. Those going through a divorce need to ask themselves the question, "Why would someone not choose to spend the rest

of their life with me?" It's a tough one. How do you think answering that question might lead to healing?

5. If you've ever been hurt by a spouse, what does that do to your ability to trust? How do you learn to trust again? What if you were the one who wasn't trustworthy? What steps could you take to become a trustworthy person?

6. Those seeking remarriage need to make sure they've healed and the person they want to marry has healed. How do you know whether or not that has happened?

7. The divorce rate for remarriages is close to 65 percent. What do you think accounts for the high rate of second marriage failure?

8. If someone wants to get remarried, what steps do you think they should take in order to build a stronger second marriage?

chapter eight

BARBIE LIVES ON

What Women Tell Me:

> *It is not always a blessing to be so thin. Hearing "Toothpick Legs" one's entire life can hurt just as much as "Thunder Thighs."*
>
> *I have always felt somewhat ugly or at least below average, but lately I have thoughts of suicide because I feel I am too ugly to be alive.*
>
> *I feel like negative body image and compulsive overeating are taking over my life.*

• • •

I DIDN'T OWN A BARBIE DOLL. I didn't even want a Barbie doll, or I didn't until I saw a commercial for Tressy, the doll with hair that grows. Just like Barbie, Tressy had the "perfect" look. Perfect complexion, perfect features, and perfect clothes, if you could afford to keep buying new outfits. The Christmas I got Tressy I think I received one additional outfit. I'm sure she was in and out of those two outfits twenty times a day.

To my six- or seven-year-old sense of fashion, though, paper dolls were king. In the world of paper dolls, I could get lost for hours at a time, and since it was only paper, I could afford to have twenty or thirty outfits. My favorite was always smartly dressed in a Jackie Kennedy–styled outfit. Every one of her outfits had a matching hat. I still like hats!

Even if you disapproved of Barbies (or your mother disapproved), the existence of the doll influenced you—and us all. "Someday I'll look like her," we said in a collective voice. For me and for many of you, the truth is ... Barbie lives on.

SEEING OVER THE AIRWAVES

One of the things I like about being in radio is people don't know what I look like day to day. I don't feel pressured to present a perfect outer image. Unless listeners have done the extra work to head to my website and view a posed photo, they build a mental picture based on my voice. When I speak at women's conferences and retreats, I often ask participants if I look like what they thought I would look like. Some say yes, some say no. Then sometimes I'll smile and quip, "Just tell me I'm thinner than you thought." This statement always gets a good laugh, but even as I say it I realize it's unnecessarily pointing to outward appearance.

What is it about our psyche that makes us so conscious of our exterior—our posterior, our anterior, our skin, our thin, our hair, our flair? Long ago I memorized the Scripture (1 Samuel 16:7) that says that God looks at the heart, but I never quite forget that man—and woman—sees and judges me by my outward appearance. I'm making great strides, working to get past this issue, but from *Midday Connection* listeners I know I'm not the only one who is forever wanting to look prettier, more fashionable, and definitely thinner.

Dove's Campaign for Real Beauty website offers a quiz that includes this question: Read this next statement and decide whether it's fact or fiction. "You are beautiful!" The website indicates that 92 percent of women respond "fiction," and 92 percent also say they want to change "at least one aspect of their appearance."[1]

Mike and I were on vacation in Door County, Wisconsin, and I was working on this book, ironically, this chapter. We went out for dinner and I decided to dress up, wear a skirt instead of jeans. On the way out of the restaurant, I asked Mike, "Do I have good-looking legs?"

Like any good man, he was slow to respond, not sure if I had set a trap. He said, "Yes. You have muscular legs."

"Is that a good thing? Do you like muscular legs?"

"Of course they're okay—they're yours, and I love you," he said.

Why did it matter to me what kind of legs I have? And how many times have I asked the same kinds of questions, looking for some validation of my physical appearance, just the right comment to make me feel better about myself? And why? Because I haven't always felt good about this body of mine, and I haven't always kept it in a healthy and wholesome balance.

A LITTLE BACKGROUND NOISE/MUSIC

"Average height and weight"—that's what the pediatrician said. There's something about the word *average* that makes me cringe. I'd rather be above average, but in the realm of height and weight, we aspire to be below average. Even as a young girl I knew that being slender, slim, trim, thin—put whatever label you want on it—that's what was desirable. My mom talked about weight a lot. She talked about health too, but it seems only the weight part of what she said stuck with me. She was always working on losing weight, maintaining weight, or watching weight. So I took up the same part-time job as I got older.

I was a stick figure of a girl up until my sophomore year in high school. Going away to boarding school and the starchy menu that followed was a contributing factor to my weight gain. I recently found an old picture from my sophomore year, and I could tell by the way I stood in the photograph that I was trying to hide my hips and give myself the most flattering pose possible. I remember being thankful I was heading to Mexico on a missions trip work team that summer, because I could work hard and lose weight before going to my new school, which I did.

I was back to boarding school and back to the same old battle in the fall, though being active in sports helped to keep my weight down. The health factor hadn't kicked in yet. I loved my junk food, especially sweets. I was in charge of buying cookies and candy for a senior class fund-raiser for a trip to Washington. We'd take the snack cart floor to floor to sell sweets. As the buyer, I always got to buy something for myself wholesale. I would buy a whole box of Chico-Stix. Remember those? They were a cross between a peanut butter log and a Zagnut candy bar. There were twenty-four of these eight-inch-long sticks in a box. When I was low on cash, I'd do a grocery store run and buy a box of sugar cubes. I still enjoy a spoonful of brown sugar when I'm baking. Needless to say, nutritional training hadn't stuck.

I really watched my weight the summer before I entered college. I definitely wanted to make a good first impression and look my best. College proved much more sedentary, not to mention a trip back into the land of starchy foods. In my room I kept my usual stash of Kit-Kats or M&M's for a quick sweet fix. I went up and down in weight ten or fifteen pounds in the course of any given year. I'd always manage to reel myself in and lose the weight in the summer. I was always motivated to look good for the next group of new students coming in. Okay, the truth was, I wanted to look good for any new guys coming to Moody. You never know when Mr. Right will spot you walking across the plaza on campus. I would watch my weight for about three weeks; then I let nature take its course (translate: I ate whatever I wanted).

After graduating in May, I had two months to lose some weight before starting rehearsals for the year-long singing tour. I had thought this through and determined that if I stayed in homes every night for a year, most of those people would fix special foods and expect you to eat them, or churches would have potluck suppers where people used real butter, real sugar, and real cream. No skimping like they might for themselves. I would be someone's "company" every night for a year. "Yikes, I've got to lose weight!" I thought. So I lost twenty-five pounds in eight weeks and began the tour quite slender and proud of myself.

As the tour began, I managed to say no to the most fattening options. But about a month in I was regularly saying yes to anything. At home for a ten-day Christmas break, my mother greeted me with, "Oh, you've gained some weight!"

At the end of the touring year, my extra forty pounds and I headed home. I think the additional weight gain in the second half of the touring year was the beginning of my "I'll show you what 'oh, you've gained some weight' looks like!" After I returned home, I didn't know what was next for me, but I decided I wanted to look good for whatever it might be, so I buckled down and lost the forty pounds. When I got the call to come work for Moody Radio, I looked good! A couple of years later when I got married, I was still motivated to look good, but a few years into a difficult marriage, the pounds started piling on.

It was a comfort to eat, but I didn't see that I was using food as comfort. I dropped some pounds before I gave birth to John in 1992. I knew there would be weight gain with pregnancy, so I thought I'd better shed some weight before I got pregnant so I wouldn't have such a big hole to dig out of after giving birth. I gained only twenty-one pounds during my pregnancy and lost all that and a few more pounds within two weeks of giving birth. Seeing my thin self in the mirror kept me motivated to stay that way for a while.

My mom and dad came to visit for a couple of weeks to help out with the baby, and then I returned with them to Kansas City for another month of help. I wasn't doing very well emotionally. I remember my mom saying, "You look so good; now don't let yourself gain it back." You guessed it ... I started packing on the pounds again. I stayed depressed for a couple of years after John's birth. Today it's known as postpartum depression, but back then it wasn't talked about and I didn't realize how badly I was suffering. I gained, lost, and gained it all back again between 1994 and 2002.

Sometime in 2002 I had Danna Demetre as a guest on *Midday Connection*. I can still remember her saying, "Just make some small changes. You need to start the day with breakfast. Have a piece of low-fat, high-fiber toast and spread a thin layer of peanut butter on it for some protein. Have a hard-boiled egg along with that if you choose. Just start with some baby steps." I remember thinking during the program, "I can do that. I can take some baby steps." The very next day, I boiled an egg and ate it. As I continued these baby steps, I lost my largest amount of weight ever, fifty pounds.

I was on the weight loss track when my divorce became final. I continued losing until I reached my goal and felt very healthy. This time instead of just working on lessening my food intake and making healthier choices, I also began exercising using a treadmill. I was definitely healthier all around. But when I reached my goal, I found it hard to find the right balance of exercise and healthy eating. Sometimes it takes awhile to settle into maintaining a healthy weight.

The Christmas after my divorce, John and I took a trip to Florida to visit my folks. Sometime during the visit my mother said, "Now don't go gaining it all back again." Like that's what I'd wanted to do every time up until now? Those words were a blast from the past, every past time I'd lost weight. I didn't see how performance driven I was. I had no idea that I was striving for perfection. I wanted to hear "Well done," not "Don't gain it back again." Anything positive might have garnered a different outcome. It shocked me that the words of my mother could still hold such power over me, now an adult woman. I didn't consciously say the words, but I lived out the "I'll show you what gaining it all back looks like!"

It didn't happen immediately, but I was beginning to gain weight when I met Mike and started dating him. He was a burger-and-fries kind of guy, which didn't help. I loved him, not his culinary choices.

I was still slender when we married, but I often tell people I was very happy for the first two years of marriage; then I realized I needed to become *healthy* and *happy*, so down the weight loss trail I went again. Only this time, I wanted it to be permanent. I didn't want this to be my story for the rest of my life ... up, down, up, down, up, down. Enough!

When it comes to body image, we pass on our body obsessions to each other like a bad cold. That's basically what my mom did. She had her own obsessions with weight and certain parts of her body she was unhappy with, and she made sure I carried on the tradition. That wasn't her goal in life, but we all know these things are more caught than taught.

I'm going to leave my story there and return to it later. My story isn't yours, and yours isn't mine, but from listeners I hear painful accounts of the toll of well-intentioned family messages. "My whole life my mom has constantly been telling me, 'Well, honey, if you lose the weight ...' I've had breasts since sixth grade, and she always disliked my shape." Or "I have been an average weight most of my life and I still can never feel comfortable about my weight because there isn't a conversation with my mother or sister that doesn't focus on how we look."

THERE'S MORE TO THE PICTURE

It's important to pay attention to the messages we give our daughters at home, both overt and covert messages. In this day and age as mothers—and as sisters in Christ—we can be the first line of defense for our daughters and friends against a media onslaught of unparalleled proportions.

When I talk about body image with a live audience, in a conference or retreat setting, I often invite three women up to the platform: one who is a teenager or in her early twenties, one who is in her thirties or forties, and one in her fifties or sixties. I interview them about issues of body image to see if there is much variance in the way women of different ages respond to the questions.

First I ask, "How much of an impact do fashion magazines have on your self-esteem?" As you can imagine, the teenage response is higher than the middle- and older-age responses. Women in their fifties and sixties want the magazines for a recipe or a specific article, though the article might be related to body image or a new kind of diet. The magazine doesn't take the same toll on the mature woman's self-esteem.

I talked to the dad of a teen girl recently who said, "It's bad enough to have to deal with fifteen-year-old hormones, but add on top of that teen magazines that intimate you're not cool enough or pretty enough unless you look like our airbrushed models, and it leaves my daughter depressed most of the time. She doesn't understand that the standard is unattainable."

We can't even go to the grocery store without magazine covers assailing our senses at the checkout counter. We can't turn on the TV without half of the commercials we watch being sexually charged, not to mention the programs themselves. The ads and catalogs that come in the mail are filled with sensual images that assault our sensibilities, images that make women feel inadequate.

We can never be thin enough, pretty enough, tall enough, have a small enough nose, right-shaped hips and thighs, perfectly sculpted calves and abs, firm enough arms, and the big one—the right size breasts! There is always someone who is in better shape and whom we perceive to be more beautiful than we are. It seems the only way to escape the comparisons is to cover ourselves from head to toe. We cannot ever measure up. Our picture of beauty needs a major overhaul.

HONESTLY, CAN WE TALK?

Another question I ask at conferences is, "Do you ever talk about body image issues with your friends or mom or sisters?" The teen girls say, "We talk about how cute this model is and how we want to look like this celebrity, but we don't go any deeper than that. It's all about what we want, even though we probably know it will never come true."

The other age groups, especially the thirties and forties, say they talk about needing to work out more, because "I'm getting a poochy belly" or "I wish I could get rid of these thighs." But there isn't any discussion about why they are obsessed with looking a certain way.

The next age bracket, the fifties and sixties, can vary in response. Sometimes it's similar to the thirties and forties; sometimes it's pointing a finger and being critical of someone else. Actually, this was common to all age brackets. The consensus was that it felt better to look at someone who was worse off, heavier, not as beautiful, than to talk about why we struggle with body image.

The thing about body image for girls and women is that we think about it constantly, but we don't often talk about it. We'll make an offhand comment about others and even ourselves, but we won't get to the root of the issue. My hope is to get women talking to each other about body image issues. For starters I suggest you answer the following questions and discuss your answers with a friend.

Grab a pencil and take this quiz. No cheating! Be honest! Check all of the following statements that apply to you:

- ☐ I'm critical of my body.
- ☐ When I look in the mirror, I first notice the parts of my body that I think are inadequate.
- ☐ When I see images of beautiful women in the media, I compare myself to them.
- ☐ When I get dressed and ready in the morning, I consider what others will think of my appearance.
- ☐ I weigh myself frequently and am emotionally affected by the result.
- ☐ The thought of being seen without makeup or my hair done is scary to me.
- ☐ When others compliment my appearance, I have a hard time believing it's true.
- ☐ When I eat in front of other people, I wonder what they are thinking about me.
- ☐ I tend to wear either clothes that are baggy to hide my

figure or tight clothes to show off my body in hopes of receiving attention.

☐ I often think, if money were no object, I would have plastic surgery in a heartbeat.

☐ If I were more beautiful, that would be the solution to some of life's challenges, like my desire for romance, relationships, career success, popularity among friends or at school, or self-esteem.

☐ I spend a significant amount of money on beauty supplies.[2]

How did you do on the quiz? Did you check more than you left unchecked? If so, you may be deeply affected by the lie that your body must fit a certain standard in order to be accepted. If so, I suggest you back up and consider a balanced view of self. What would it look like? On what would it be founded?

FOUNDATIONAL VIEWS

We can return to the very beginning, where we started in chapter 1, with the biblical creation account in Genesis 1. On the sixth day, "God created human beings in his own image, in the image of God he created them; male and female he created them" (Genesis 1:27 TNIV). Every previous day Scripture calls the day's creation "good." On the sixth day? "It was very good" (v. 31).

No getting around it, whether male or female, we were made in the image of God. It doesn't get any better than that! Some of us can hardly believe that God's Word doesn't say, "God created women in the image of Angelina Jolie, Elizabeth Taylor, Tyra Banks, or Julia Roberts." You fill in the blank with a celebrity image that comes to your mind. God created us in his image. Yes, we have a soul, and yes, we were created as sexual beings, and yes, we have imagination and intelligence. The whole person is important. We've just skewed the importance meter way over to the body side of things.

When you are tempted to be overly critical of your body, tell yourself a foundational truth—you are created by God in the "very good" category. What's more, "Do you not know that your body is a temple of the Holy Spirit, who is in you, whom you have received from God?" (1 Corinthians 6:19). What does that mean? He lives in us. He knows us. He loves us.

Psalm 139 is a favorite of mine because I've struggled to believe that God loves me. When I need to be reminded of his love, I read the first eighteen verses of Psalm 139 and insert my name where I read personal pronouns. I ask you to try this. Every time there is a personal pronoun, insert your name. To make this easy for you, I've taken the liberty of putting blanks in the scriptural passage everywhere there is a personal pronoun. I've also adjusted the tenses and a word here or there to make grammatical sense. Just write your name into those blanks and read Psalm 139 aloud:

¹ *O LORD, you have examined _____ heart*
and know everything about _____.
² *You know when _____ sits down or stands up.*
You know _____ thoughts even when _____ is far
away.
³ *You see _____ when _____ travels*
and when _____ rests at home.
You know everything _____ does.
⁴ *You know what _____ is going to say*
even before _____ says it, LORD.
⁵ *You go before _____ and follow _____.*
You place your hand of blessing on _____ head.
⁶ *Such knowledge is too wonderful for _____,*

too great for _____ to understand!
7 *_____ can never escape from your Spirit!*
_____ can never get away from your presence!
8 *If _____ goes up to heaven, you are there;*
if _____ goes down to the grave, you are there.
9 *If _____ rides the wings of the morning,*
if _____ dwells by the farthest oceans,
10 *even there your hand will guide _____,*
and your strength will support _____.
11 *_____ could ask the darkness to hide _____*
and the light around _____ to become night—
12 *but even in darkness _____ cannot hide from you.*
To you the night shines as bright as day.
Darkness and light are the same to you.
13 *You made all the delicate, inner parts of _____ body*
and knit _____ together in _____ mother's womb.
14 *Thank you for making _____ so wonderfully complex!*
Your workmanship is marvelous—how well _____
  knows it.
15 *You watched _____ as _____ was being formed in*
  utter seclusion,
as _____ was woven together in the dark of the womb.
16 *You saw _____ before _____ was born.*
Every day of _____ life was recorded in your book.
Every moment was laid out
before a single day had passed.
17 *How precious are your thoughts about _____, O God.*
They cannot be numbered!
18 *_____ can't even count them;*
they outnumber the grains of sand!
And when _____ wakes up,
you are still with _____! (NLT)

When I have a woman stand and read Psalm 139 at a conference, putting her name in the blanks, often she is in tears before she can finish the passage. When we personalize Scripture passages like this one, when we read with what I call sacred imagination to engage with Scripture, we take what could have been a routine reading and make it our own. Compound that with the moving of God's Spirit as we read Scripture, and we get to see God's power in action.

God created me. He knows me. He loves me. I can't emphasize this point enough. Here's another scriptural confirmation: "When I consider your heavens, the work of your fingers, the moon and the stars, which you have set in place, what is man that you are mindful of him, the son of man that you care for him? You made him a little lower than the heavenly beings and crowned him with glory and honor" (Psalm 8:3–5). Commenting on that passage, Sheila Walsh writes, "We live in a world that stands in awe of very little. But stop for a moment and reflect. The God of the universe has chosen you to know him! It's like crawling out of a ditch covered in mud and debris and being put on the best-dressed list."[3]

A few pages later Sheila Walsh says something that startled me. Her topic is self-absorption and she writes, "When you feel that everyone around you is more capable, more attractive, more lovable, you may think that you esteem them higher but in reality you despise them. It's only when we can receive the love of God for ourselves that we can rejoice at the beauty of God in others."[4]

HONORING GOD WITH A BALANCED LIFE

Earlier I quoted 1 Corinthians where Paul says our bodies are the temple of the Holy Spirit. The next verse continues, "You are not your own; you were bought at a price. Therefore honor God with your body" (1 Corinthians 6:20). The body God chose for each of us, our eyes, our hair, our breasts, our hips, our thighs, is actually not ours. Who we are, the whole package, mind, body, soul, is a tool for God's kingdom. In context Paul is talking about sexual relations, but I see parallels for us as we consider a balanced view — neither obsessively self-absorbed nor neglectful — of our physical bodies.

There is a healthy place somewhere between body obsession and body neglect, and we have to be vigilant to find that place and live in it. Sometimes when we can't obtain what we believe is the ideal, we let ourselves go and cease to care about our appearance. That is body neglect. Body obsession manifests itself in eating disorders, which are often centered in issues of control. We need to come before God daily, maybe even minute by minute, and ask him to show us when our behaviors manifest body obsession and when they reflect body neglect.

Let me clarify a few points. Am I saying we shouldn't care a lick how we look? Am I suggesting you throw out all your makeup? Not at all. We've bought into the lie that role models are the same as cover models. They're not! As Christian women honoring God, we would do well to be conscious of our appearance. It's okay to look good, just not okay to be obsessed with looking good. A listener relates this well when she describes her mother: "She told me I was pretty, but she spent a lot more time encouraging me with skills and character, so my confidence came much more from the skills and talents with which I could serve the Lord, rather than obsessing with the many physical imperfections I have."

Am I saying that if we've "got it" we should flaunt it? Not at all. Sometimes the way we choose to dress becomes a distraction whereby we invite others to worship our body instead of pointing to God. Sometimes we use the beauty we've been given to get what we think we are missing. If we are starving for love, we try to look for it in all the wrong places and through the wrong means. *Modesty* is the word I'll use here, a word that's gotten a bad rap. You're probably thinking a grandma in a rocker with her blouse buttoned up to her chin. Sometimes we don't have a clue and need a friend to help us in the area of modesty. Dannah Gresh has written a great little book called *Secret Keeper: The Delicate Power of Modesty*. If you have daughters or have struggled with the issue of modesty, I highly recommend this great resource.

MAKING HEALTHY CHANGES

There is another question I ask live conference audiences: "Do you exercise to stay a certain weight, or so you'll keep physically fit?" Many women think exercise is simply a means of weight control. The truth is that we need to keep our bodies healthy and in good shape. This has a huge impact on us the older we get.

Two years ago, a visit to my doctor jolted me. My cholesterol had gone up and my doctor told me I was too young to be on cholesterol medication. She said, "I want to see you in six weeks, and if you haven't lost some weight, I'm going to take drastic measures." I didn't want to know what her measures were, so I started on the path of healthy eating and began to exercise. As a first step, I cut my food consumption in half. Then I added exercise. I began by doing twenty sit-ups morning and evening, along with stretching. I know that doesn't sound like much, but when you're forty to fifty pounds overweight, you have to start slow. Just stretching and doing sit-ups winded me.

Then I began making healthier food choices along with controlling portion size. Baked versus fried, margarine versus butter, canola oil versus vegetable oil. It was all about making wise food choices. It wasn't a drastic change. I found a breakfast bar that was higher in fiber but contained my favorites, peanuts and chocolate. I found another bar that had chocolate and pretzels in it that also worked as a nice low-calorie dessert. I added more vegetables into the mix, and I became a big fan of Lean Cuisine, Smart Ones, and Healthy Choice meals.

As my physical stamina increased, I began bike riding. In nice weather I rode on local trails. In inclement or cold weather, I went to the health club or used my Gazelle machine at home. I did my sit-ups and stretches daily, now numbering fifty sit-ups; I did other more aerobic exercise a minimum of three times a week. No magic diet, just plain old hard work and discipline.

At about the six-week mark, I had lost sixteen pounds and the doctor was amazed and happy. Me too!

I WANT A BLIZZARD!

Around the same time, I had a defining moment. I have an old dining room set. It was my maternal grandparents' from back on the farm in northern Maine. My mom passed it on to me and said, "I always want you to have this." I've moved a couple of times since she gave me the set, and each time she'd ask if the house I was considering had a dining room in it. I remember asking once, "Mom, what do I do if the house I buy doesn't have a dining room?" She responded, "I'm sure you'll find one with a dining room." I wasn't so sure.

My current home does have a dining room, but when I remarried, my husband and I made it into a family room. We moved the dining room table and buffet into the great room, which is also a living room. It was a bit crowded, but we made it work. Here's the thing: we're not dining-room-table kind of folk. We often eat around the coffee table. Even when we invite guests in, we'll do a buffet type of meal, or a meal of hors d'oeuvres. Twice we've hosted house concerts where we moved all of our furniture to the edges of our great room to accommodate about fifty people for an evening of music.

Mike said to me one day, "We really could use the space the dining room table takes up."

"I agree, but what will Mom say?" I couldn't bring myself to sell the dining room set; neither did I want to pay for storage. I didn't know what to do until one day I woke up with a clear mind and said, "This is our house and we're going to have the furniture that we want to use where we want to use it." And so I figured out how to take the old dining room table apart to store it in our basement until I decided what to do with it.

As Mike and I dismantled the table, I began to feel extreme sadness. I didn't know why. Many of you know how important a daughter's relationship is with her mother. You've experienced it, the good and the bad. These are strong, sometimes painful ties. In my case, my mother's word was gospel. She held strong opinions and I usually abided by her word. Often her counsel was stellar, brilliant, and extremely helpful. But there were those other moments. And I was experiencing one of them.

In the midst of carrying the dining room table to the basement piece by piece, I began to cry. I called for Mike, laid my head on his shoulder, and sobbed. Through my sobs I tried to talk. At first Mike couldn't understand a word I said. I tried again. "I want a Blizzard."

"What do you want?"

"I want a Dairy Queen Blizzard."

"What are you talking about? That seems odd. You're sobbing and you want to go to DQ?"

"Yes," I said, crying even more loudly. I wanted more than anything else in that moment to get in the car and drive to the local Dairy Queen for a Blizzard. I didn't want just any Blizzard—I wanted a Butterfinger Blizzard. Up to that point I never thought I turned to food as comfort. I had given this issue thought on many occasions. I always thought I just didn't exercise enough and that I struggled with eating too much, nothing more, nothing less. For the first time I saw it. I felt it at my core. I wanted food more than Jesus. I didn't want to go to God with my sadness; I wanted a DQ Blizzard and I wanted it bad.

With a tearstained face and in a broken voice, I sobbed to Mike, "I am so sad, and I'm so ashamed. I want food more than Jesus. I see it for the first time ever."

Like a good man he said, "That's okay. It'll be okay." And for several minutes he just held me and listened. But being a guy, and not able to stop himself, he slowly worked his way into offering a solution. He said, "Why don't you take a little break and fix yourself a snack?"

Then I knew he hadn't heard a word I said. Of course, when I cry, I barely utter anything coherent, so I can't come down on him too hard. He was trying to be helpful, but he really *hadn't* heard me. I was crying and he wanted it to stop! I knew he just wanted me to feel better, but this was one of those moments when I needed to sit in the sadness and cry on Jesus' shoulder. I didn't need a quick-fix male solution. After I prayed and confessed my sin, I felt the arms of my Savior wrap around me in such a loving way. It wasn't tangible, but I knew he felt my pain and had forgiven my sin.

AN ONGOING CONVERSATION

I haven't arrived when it comes to food, but I lost forty-five pounds. Yes, forty-five pounds. I'm within normal weight guidelines for my height and age. What's more, for the first time I've not gained my weight back. And I have great confidence that I'm going to keep it off. You see, I have an ongoing conversation with God about food, and more often than not, I run to him when

I'm struggling, rather than to food. It was a long journey and a lot of pounds gained and lost. Not coincidentally, the center of this battle with food was the dismantling of a dining room table. God's kindness or God's sense of humor? Probably a little of both.

I highly recommend an ongoing conversation with God through prayer, through Scripture, and through journaling. Scripture memory can be key. Pick out a couple of verses from Psalm 139 and commit them to memory with your name interjected into the text.

The conversation doesn't have to take place only when you're journaling. It might take place when you feel depressed as you scrutinize your face in the mirror. Maybe you're like the listener who said she was "becoming obsessed with the wrinkles on her face." Maybe after you've gone to buy a new pair of pants and found that you're up a size, you've gone on a retail therapy spree instead of to Jesus. Start a dialogue with God instead of whatever you've done in the past. Don't let your feelings get the best of you; stand on the facts of who you are in Christ.

LIKE ESTHER ...

In our obsession with externals, we forget that beauty can only take us so far. In Esther 2:7 we read, "Esther was lovely in form and features." Because of her beauty, "the king was attracted to Esther more than to any of the other women, and she won his favor and approval more than any of the other virgins. So he set a royal crown on her head and made her queen" (Esther 2:17). As time passed the king didn't call for Esther as frequently. Her beauty won her the royal crown but didn't keep her in the king's presence. Esther had likely relied on her beauty most of her life. She knew how to please people too. Scripture says, "Esther won the favor of everyone who saw her" (Esther 2:15).

The major turn in the story comes when Haman — let's call him the prime minister — decrees that all of the Jews be annihilated. Virtually no one knows that Esther is a Jew, and her cousin Mordecai sends word that she must go into the king's presence and beg for mercy for her people. Esther is understandably afraid. No one, not even the queen, goes to the king's court without being summoned. The penalty is death unless the king extends the gold scepter, indicating that the visitor may come forward. She doesn't give Mordecai much reason for hope. "Thirty days have passed since I was called to go to the king," she declares (Esther 4:11).

Then Mordecai utters these famous words: "Do not think that because you are in the king's house you alone of all the Jews will escape. For if you remain silent at this time, relief and deliverance for the Jews will arise from another place, but you and your father's family will perish. And who knows but that you have come to royal position for such a time as this?" (Esther 4:13–14). This seems to be a defining moment for Esther. She moves from girl to woman. She takes charge. She no longer relies on her beauty but becomes a woman of courage. She no longer listens to Mordecai's words; he listens to her instructions and carries them out.

All the tension is taken out of the story for us because we know how it ends. Remember that as she approached the king, Esther didn't know whether or not she would live. As Carolyn Custis James wrote, "Until the crisis, Esther lived by the culture's view of who she was and what gave her value. No one looked beneath the surface. No one wondered what gifts God had entrusted to Esther, what vital contributions she was supposed to make."[5]

Esther was more than a pretty face, and God was about to show her what she was made of. Carolyn Custis James continues,

"God wanted more from Esther. He actually put her in a position that compelled her to become a bold, courageous adventurer and do some rescuing of her own. Not only was no one there to take care of her, she had to defend a nation."[6]

Does God want more from me? Does God want more from you? What might making a courageous stand for him look like in your world? What is God calling you to do? If we are consumed by our outward appearance, we can easily miss the bigger picture. Make no mistake: God wants to use you for kingdom purposes, just as he used Esther. Are you ready?

DISCUSSION QUESTIONS

1. Body image is something most women don't talk to each other about, often because it is a point of much pain. How could it be mutually healing to bring this discussion out in the open with other women?

2. Can you point to a time in your childhood when someone shamed you for the way you looked? How did that make you feel then? Now?

3. If that was true for you, how have you carried that shame? Negative self-talk? Slouching posture? Other ways?

4. Do you ever find yourself wearing baggy clothing to hide your body, or tight clothing to show off your body? Why do you think that is?

5. Do you find yourself running to food, feeling depressed, or wanting to shop to avoid dealing with difficult feelings that arise due to body image issues?

6. Sometimes we recognize after the fact how we've avoided God. Can you think of a time when you ran to a counterfeit comforter instead of Jesus?

chapter nine

I LOVE TO TELL
THE STORY

What Women Tell Me:
 My husband and I are in our midfifties
and love to spend time discipling younger people.
However, I am not without my moments of won-
dering what my purpose is now that the children
are grown.
 When we retired we wanted to do short-term
mission work. We just ask the Lord to lead us and
show us where we could serve.

• • •

I GREW UP ATTENDING SUNDAY EVENING services. To be honest, when I was a child, Sundays weren't my favorite day of the
week. I enjoyed Sunday school, but then I had to sit still and
be quiet in the big people's church service. I loved Sunday dinner, because at our house it was always hamburgers and chips.

That was our tradition. I wasn't fond of our mandatory Sunday afternoon nap. And I really wasn't interested in heading back to church at night where, once again, I had to sit still and be quiet. There was one exception, and I lived for it. I dearly loved to sing, and the fifth Sunday night of every month was a hymn sing. There are not nearly enough fifth Sundays on the calendar.

If you've never attended a hymn sing, it is as it sounds, a whole church service devoted to singing hymns. Some are chosen by the song leader, but there is always a period of time set aside to take favorites from the congregation. I was a shy little girl, but at the hymn sing I learned to be bold. I learned to shout out the numbers of my favorite hymns or risk having to wait until another fifth Sunday to sing them.

I had four or five on my favorites list. Hymns like "Wonderful Grace of Jesus," "When the Roll Is Called Up Yonder," "He Keeps Me Singing," and "I Love to Tell the Story." Some I picked for their melody, and some I picked for their lyrics. The meaning of all of these favorites grew deeper as I got older. "I Love to Tell the Story" speaks to me in new ways today. The fourth verse reads,

> *I love to tell the story, for those who know it best*
> *Seem hungering and thirsting to hear it like the rest.*
> *And when, in scenes of glory, I sing the new, new song,*
> *'Twill be the old, old story, that I have loved so long.*

After I accepted Christ into my life, there came a time when I experienced what author Alan Kraft calls "gospel drift." Maybe you have too. "Every one of us is vulnerable to this gospel drift in our spiritual lives. Without realizing it, we stop hearing the melodies of brokenness and faith and instead begin pursuing a spirituality of self-effort and self-sufficiency."[1]

Thank God crisis hit my life! As a result, the old, old story once again became to me a new, new song. Jesus helped me recover my life. He took me back to that wonderful moment when I first found him. In that moment, "we hear the melody of *brokenness* — that we are sinners desperately in need of a Savior. And we hear the melody of *faith* — that there is an all-sufficient Savior named Jesus who paid the price we couldn't pay, who lived the life we couldn't live."[2] I love to tell that story!

In these pages you've read portions of my story as it relates to themes and concerns of listeners to *Midday Connection*. My story isn't yours, and yet we are intricately related as Christians — members of Christ's body, the church. In 1 Corinthians 12 Paul says, "The eye cannot say to the hand, 'I don't need you!' And the head cannot say to the feet, 'I don't need you!' " He continues, "If one part suffers, every part suffers with it; if one part is honored, every part rejoices with it. Now you are the body of Christ, and each one of you is a part of it" (vv. 21, 26–27).

Each of you is a part of it, and each of you has a story to tell. Sometimes women say, "I don't have any kind of story worth telling or hearing." I often hear that sentiment from someone like me who had a childhood conversion. I came to Christ at age seven. It happened during a week of evangelistic meetings. At the end of the evangelist's sermon one night, I felt the tug of the Holy Spirit, and the next thing I knew I was walking down the aisle to ask Jesus into my life.

But our conversion story is only a small piece of our timeline. Picture a long piece of rope strung as a clothesline from one end of your house or apartment to the other. Then picture a tiny black dot somewhere on the rope. That dot is the span of your life in relationship to eternity. And your conversion story is a tiny molecule on the black dot. The bigger question is what happened before or after that moment of conversion that marked you as a person. Where has your journey of faith taken you?

What is the theme God is writing on your life — or mine? Discovering that theme helps us move into the future with a real sense of purpose. If we are going to uncover the masterpiece that we are, we have to know our story. "For we are God's masterpiece. He has created us anew in Christ Jesus, so we can do the good things he planned for us long ago" (Ephesians 2:10 NLT).

Vinita Hampton Wright says, "Your soul has been spinning stories since the day you were born."[3] Our story is not about a onetime event. It's about the faith journey we're on. God doesn't treat us like puppets, pulling our strings. We are wondrously interdependent beings who are called to co-write our story with God. And God uses all parts of our story for his glory. He even, maybe especially, uses our pain and brokenness.

Sitting in my office one Thursday, I had two unexpected interactions. The first was with Joe. He is *Midday Connection*'s Friday 4 special features producer. Joe stepped in to tell me that his wife had just been diagnosed with breast cancer. He said, "We're on a new journey now. Who knew when we were doing those interviews at the Cardinal Bernadin Cancer Center at Loyola Center for Health that we'd need the services of the people we talked with?" Joe walked with me through the hard waters of divorce just ten years ago; now it was my turn to walk beside Joe and his wife on a different journey. They are going to have things to say to a totally new group of people because of their experience.

The other interaction was through email and phone with a friend trying to extricate herself from a codependent relationship. "It is painful and lonely," she said. I listened and offered a couple of thoughts; mostly I listened. She knows the answers but has to live through the relational pain. She talked to me because I've been there. I've experienced codependency.

If I believe that God, in part, writes our stories for the benefit of others, then I have an opportunity to speak up and share out of my brokenness to help others in the body of Christ. I honestly can say I have learned to love my own story, as I've seen how it enables me to intersect with the pain of others.

You've read about my struggle as a Pharisee and my journey toward knowing myself. I think it's critical in our growth as Christ followers to talk about authenticity with ourselves because it leads to authenticity with God. Knowing myself led to the healing of my image of God. When I found out I was performance driven, I realized I believed God loved me only when I performed well, something I wouldn't have discovered without self-awareness. Knowing ourselves more deeply often leads to knowing God more deeply. And of course when we know God more deeply, he opens up all kinds of doors and windows to know ourselves more deeply. And when that begins to happen, our journey starts to become a holy journey.

Luci Shaw notes, "It is not insignificant that much of the Bible ... is narrative in form and that the characters and plots revealed on the sacred pages are not so different from those that surround and involve us today."[4] Jesus knew the importance of telling stories and parables; so did the gospel writers as they give us glimpses into the personal encounters of Jesus' life.

I WAS BLIND BUT NOW I SEE

John 9 relates the story of the healing of a man who was blind from birth. Jesus' disciples see the blind man by the side of the road and ask Jesus why he was born blind. Was it because of his parents' sin? Or his own sin? Jesus puts a stop to that reasoning and says, "This happened so that the work of God might be displayed in his life. As long as it is day, we must do the work of him who sent me. Night is coming, when no one can work.

While I am in the world, I am the light of the world" (John 9:3–5). What an interesting statement for Jesus to make in the context of talking to a blind man. This is someone who has never seen light, either physical or spiritual. His life was about to change.

Then what does Jesus do? He spits in the dirt, makes mud with his saliva, and puts the mud on the man's eyes. He tells the man to go to the Pool of Siloam (which means "sent") and wash his face. Could you imagine having this miracle worker called Jesus, whom you'd heard about, approach you, put mud on your eyes and tell you to wash, and then wondering, "When I do what he tells me, will I really be able to see?"

What do you think it was like for him? When he first opened his eyes, was his vision fuzzy for a few moments while images and colors came into focus? Did he stagger in awe of sights never seen before? I can only imagine. One thing we do know from the written account, he was asked repeatedly about this Man who had healed him. Even his parents were called to confirm: Is this your son, the one who was blind? "Yes", they replied, "he's our son, but we don't know how he became sighted. He's an adult; ask him!"

And what was the man's final claim? He said he didn't know exactly who Jesus was. "Whether he is a sinner or not, I don't know. One thing I do know. I was blind but now I see!" (John 9:25). As the Life Application Study Bible notes say, "He didn't know how or why he had been healed, but he knew that his life had been miraculously changed, and he was not afraid to tell the truth."

You don't need to know all the answers in order to share Christ with others. It's important just to tell people how he has changed your life; it's important to tell them your story. Then trust that God will use your words to help others believe in him.

You don't have to be a Bible scholar. You just need to know and have experienced the truth of John 9:25: "One thing I do know. I was blind but now I see!"

RECLAIMING YOUR TRUE NAME

I want to point you toward knowing and understanding your own story so that who you truly are can be allowed to shine for all to see. And through your shining, God will draw women and men to himself. "For what we preach is not ourselves, but Jesus Christ as Lord, and ourselves as your servants for Jesus' sake. For God, who said, 'Let light shine out of darkness,' made his light shine in our hearts to give us the light of the knowledge of God's glory displayed in the face of Christ" (2 Corinthians 4:5–6 TNIV).

Think back to your childhood. Did you have a nickname? Was it humorous? Was it hurtful? Some of you are carrying around a name that wounds you every time you hear it or think it. Who gave it to you? Classmates? Siblings? A parent? Did it stick? Do you still have it today? Is it a private or public nickname?

I was named "perfect." As I said in chapter 1, I overheard my mother say, "She's an angel. Sometimes I wonder if she's a dream, if she'll be gone one day when I go to her room to get her up in the morning." I'm sure some of you can identify with that "naming." That was an incredible weight to put on a child. I spent decades trying to live up to that name.

One reason we end up putting on masks of perfection is because we choose to become what others expect us to be. Living up to other people's expectations is a sure way to stay distanced from our authentic selves. "People pleasing"—it's why I tried to be perfect for so long. I did what I "ought" to do based on the expectations of others, based on the "name" my mother gave me.

What's in a name? For one thing, it's an identifier. Think about why your name is used. I remember hoping my name would be passed over for jury duty, but I had to wait and listen. I was with my teenage son to see the smile appear on his face when he heard "John Lustrea" called out to signify that his driver's license was ready for pickup. I remember as a kid hearing, "Anita Belle Fore, get in here!" You knew you were in trouble when first, middle, and last name were called out by a parent.

I've had women come up to me at retreats to say, "I still call myself 'thunder thighs' because my brothers called me that over and over. That name has been embedded in my mind. I hate the way I look because of that." Or "I despise my name because every time I hear someone say it, I remember my dad and the way he said my name before he would sexually abuse me." Or "I remember the kids calling me Ssssstuttering SSSSSusan, and I wanted to crawl in a hole." The memory of our names, both nicknames and real names, can cause deep pain. That's why it is so important to know, beyond a shadow of a doubt, that God knows our true names.

In the story of Naomi, we see that we sometimes try to change our names. "'Don't call me Naomi,' she told them. 'Call me Mara [Bitter], because the Almighty has made my life very bitter.... Why call me Naomi? The Lord has afflicted me; the Almighty has brought misfortune upon me'" (Ruth 1:20–21). But God didn't discard Naomi. He knew her true name. What does it mean for God to know our true names?

First, God knows us intimately. Consider Matthew 10:30: "And even the very hairs of your head are all numbered." Isaiah

49:16 reminds us that God keeps our names ever before him. "See, I have engraved you on the palms of my hands."

Second, because he calls us by name, we are able to recognize his voice. "He calls his own sheep by name and leads them out. When he has brought out all his own, he goes on ahead of them, and his sheep follow him because they know his voice. But they will never follow a stranger; in fact, they will run away from him because they do not recognize a stranger's voice" (John 10:3–5).

Often when our world rips apart, we are able to see more easily what our story is and to hear more clearly what our true names are. One ultimate comforting fact about God knowing our names is that if we are Christ followers, we know, as Luke 10:20 says, "that [our] names are written in heaven." That's the definitive knowing of our names. Our names are inscribed in heaven and we are assured of eternity with him. As you join God in authoring your story, you can discard all but your true name because of God's healing power.

As we are willing, God in his grace moves us along on the faith continuum in all kinds of ways, not the least of which is through the crises that come into our lives. As the experience of the blind man showed, the crises or hardships in our lives happen so the work of God might be displayed.

FILL IN THE BLANKS

Before you read on, grab some paper and think about how you would fill in the blanks, using this pattern:

> *I was blind, but now I see! I was _____,*
> *but now I _____.*

What were you named in the past? Are you still living that "ought" kind of existence? Do you cling to a mask of perfection?

A mask of bitterness? Take a few minutes to think about how you would fill in these blanks.

John Newton, a onetime slave trader who became an influential clergyman, used the pattern to tell his story: "I once was lost but now am found." I could answer in several ways: "I was chained in a prison filled with fear of letting God down, but now I'm free." Or "I once thought I was perfect, but now I know I'm a mess." Or "I once relied on my own devices, but now I rely on God." Or "I was afraid, but now I'm at peace." There are so many ways to fill in those blanks. You might need to think in future tense, turning the phrase into a prayer, asking God to move you in a certain direction or to work in your heart over a specific issue. The transformation might not be a reality yet. Sometimes we see where we want to be, but we're still a long way off. God's grace helps us cover the distance.

Women tell me they've filled in the blanks this way: "I was a gossip, and now I'm a pray-er." "I was a complainer, and now I'm filled with gratitude." The transformation and healing you have experienced—or that you acknowledge the need for—are part of your story. I encourage you to share your story with someone. Our faith is deepened when we hear what God has done in the lives of our brothers and sisters in Christ. Telling our stories to each other builds up our faith.

THE THEME OF YOUR LIFE

As we prayerfully consider our life stories, themes emerge. One theme has become clear to me in recent years. But I'll start the story back in my school days. In high school and in college, we didn't have dances or proms; we had banquets. We dressed up and sat at large round tables; ate lemon pepper chicken breasts, green beans, and baked potatoes; and listened to motivational speakers. The schools I attended required us to adhere to behavioral pledges. We weren't allowed to drink, dance, smoke, or chew. Or, as the wisecrack saying goes, "hang around those who do." Even now as an employee of a parachurch organization, I am expected to follow lifestyle rules. So I've lived most of my life with imposed constraints.

Don't get me wrong. There were marvelous things about the stream of evangelicalism that I grew up in. I'm so grateful for the foundational faith and theology I gained in my young years. I remember interviewing Lisa Beamer, Todd Beamer's wife, on *Midday Connection* soon after September 11, 2001. I'll never forget when she said she wasn't sure she could have handled that fateful day and the ensuing firestorm if she hadn't laid that firm foundation of faith long before United Flight 93 crashed into that Pennsylvania field on 9/11. As a girl and young woman, I knew in whom I believed. I learned to love the Word of God. I memorized hundreds of Scripture verses in vacation Bible school and in Sunday school. I grew up memorizing the hymn book. I didn't, however, grow up understanding much about God's grace and freedom.

DANCING IN GOD'S GRACE

Thankfully, because I belong to Christ and have opened myself up to him, he is constantly putting me in places where I'm being challenged and changed. Let me fast-forward to the summer I was dating Mike, who was the pastor of single adults — the Ascend ministry — at our church. I had been dating him for several months when I decided to venture out and go with him to an informal gathering of about seventy single men and women — Ascend folk.

They were going to hear Aretha Franklin at Ravinia, an impressive outdoor concert venue in the suburban north shore of Chicago. Since 1904 Ravinia has been Chicago's "sound of summer." It is a beautiful outdoor venue where you can hear musical greats from the Chicago Symphony to Harry Connick Jr. People arrive with blankets to spread on the ground, folding chairs to set up, picnic dinners and little tables along with candelabras and wine and cheese.... It's quite a romantic setting out under the stars. Mike picked me up, and we drove to the church. In the car Mike casually commented, "Don't be surprised if one of the guys from Ascend asks you to dance or grabs your hands and pulls you to your feet to dance."

Remember, I had *never* danced; dancing was not an acceptable form of entertainment in my world. "What are you talking about?" I exclaimed. "I can't, I don't know how, I don't want to." I felt panicked. Terrified.

At the church we met up with Bob, an older man (he could easily have been my dad) and his girlfriend, Ursula, to carpool. At Ravinia the large group broke into groups of eight or ten. I remember thinking, "There's not much room to dance with this sold-out crowd," but I could still see some patches of grass for dancing that gave me pause. I tried to forget about it as Ursula pulled out her china plates for us to use. Yes, china, also a Ravinia tradition. Nothing is done halfway at Ravinia.

We unwrapped our turkey and cheese deli sandwiches and passed around tortilla chips and spicy salsa. After an hour or so of chatting while we cleaned up the dinner mess and pulled out chocolate chip cookies and apple pie, Aretha started belting it out. I was having a marvelous time glued to my chair. Then she transitioned into an up-tempo song that brought the crowd to its feet. Bob grabbed my hands and tried to pull me up to dance. Do you know what I did? I pulled back. I thought, "Bob is not going to understand if I say, 'I work at a conservative Christian institution and I don't think it's appropriate if I dance.'" I kept pulling back on Bob's hands. I pulled so hard, I can't believe he didn't end up in my lap.

I looked over at Mike hoping for a rescue. He just sat there with a big smile on his face. He said nothing and did nothing, then turned and looked away. Finally in an exasperated tone Bob said, "Well, you can at least clap and sway to the music, can't you?"

I thought, "Yeah, I can do that." So Bob pulled me up and I stood and clapped and swayed — but minimally. When the last note of the song hit, you've never seen someone sit down in a chair so fast. I sat down thinking I had danced — not that I had moved my feet. I was quite smug, actually. I had this sense that I'd beat the system. Danced without really dancing. Remember when you were little and you thought you'd gotten away with something? Remember how self-satisfied you felt? I felt a little guilty, but not too much. Certainly I felt altogether too many emotions running through me for such a silly thing as dancing.

Here is the clincher. Because I stood up and minimally swayed and clapped to the music, something started happening in my heart. I didn't even realize it initially. On the way back to my house, I explained to Mike what happened with Bob. I intended to give him a hard time for not coming to my rescue, but instead I began to cry (a man's worst nightmare). "Where is this coming from?" I wondered. In fact, for days, every time I tried to talk to Mike or other friends about this experience, I started to cry. I said to Mike, "I think something significant happened in me because of Bob pulling me to my feet to dance." But I couldn't articulate exactly what happened, or what was beginning to happen.

The following Wednesday, in God's gracious plan, I had Larry Crabb scheduled as a guest on *Midday Connection*. I decided to ask Larry if he had a couple of extra minutes to talk.

So I related the Ravinia story to him and, again, started to cry. He asked, "Anita, did you dance?" I wasn't exactly sure if he was going to berate me or praise me. I said, through my tears, "As much as I knew how, yes, I danced." Larry said, "Good, because inside, your soul is dancing like crazy, and your body just has to catch up to it."

He kept talking. "You know what my wife, Rachel, and I have done for the last couple of years? We've taken dance lessons, because my sixtieth birthday party was a dance."

It was as if the chains fell off, or at least began to fall off. My conversation with Larry was healing on many levels. After I shared about the Ravinia experience, I talked to him about the pain of going through a divorce as a public figure in a conservative organization and how God was starting to open me up to his grace and freedom and heal the distorted image of God that I'd held on to for so many years. I had held so long to the belief that God loved me only if I performed well for him. I wasn't sure if I could stop living as if his love was conditional, as if he only extended his hand of grace to me if I was the perfect child, always following the rules. Larry's life-giving words continued to help dismantle these distortions I believed.

The next words out of Larry's mouth have never left me. In fact, on my desk I have a framed picture of a beautiful galloping horse, given to me by Dee Brestin, as a reminder of Larry's words. Larry said, "Anita, this is the picture that's coming to my mind about you. You are this beautiful mare that has been confined in a horse trailer; you've been pulled around in that horse trailer for years, but someone has just opened the back gate, and you've come out of that trailer and you're free. You're just learning how to run."

LIVING INTO A NEW NAME

That was the beginning of a new kind of life for me. A life where I began to live into a new name. Instead of "perfect," I was named "free." I realized more deeply that God's purpose for me was to communicate freedom to women, but I could only communicate it as deeply as I'd experienced it. I thank God for Larry's life-giving words that day!

A few months later I saw Larry Crabb in person. I was a part of one of his seminars, telling a piece of my story. When we broke for lunch, a small group of us were scheduled to eat with Larry. When he walked into our lunchroom and saw me, he grabbed my hands, swung my arms, and twirled me around as we danced right there in the basement of the church. "I once was chained and in bondage, and now I'm free." How would you fill in the blanks?

Here's the bottom line. This has nothing to do with whether I dance or not, or whether I "do" anything else. You fill in the blank with the behavioral issue of your choice. This is, as Galatians 5:1 says, about freedom in Christ: "It is for freedom that Christ has set us free. Stand firm, then, and do not let yourselves be burdened again by a yoke of slavery."

Lest you think I'm talking about unbridled license, let me explain. Those of us who grew up in conservative Christian circles get so caught up in the "letter of the law" that we can become Pharisees. In Galatians 5:13–14 Paul goes on to say, "You, my brothers and sisters, were called to be free. But do not use your freedom to indulge the sinful nature; rather, serve one another humbly in love. For the entire law is fulfilled in keeping this one command: 'Love your neighbor as yourself'" (TNIV). In my circles we became legalistic about playing cards, attending movies, dancing, and other such things. For you it might be something totally different, but the principle is the same.

When we step into the stream of God's grace, there are still riverbanks; it isn't a free-for-all. It doesn't turn into an ocean with no boundaries. Lilias Trotter, the British artist who spent her life as a missionary in Algeria, expressed this wonderful truth as she looked out at the Alps on vacation there. "The milky-looking glacier torrent spoke with God's voice this morning — so obedient to its course in its narrow bed, yet just tossing with freedom and swing in every motion. Such a picture of the 'rivers of living water' — bound and yet unbound."[5]

This was a spiritual issue, a spiritual awakening within me. And this is a significant piece of my story. The overarching theme of my life is to communicate freedom to women. That might be through the freeing message of the gospel that Christ died for us to give us a fresh start, a new life. That through entering into relationship with him, we are indeed new creations. That message will take various forms. There is freedom when we live authentically in community and start knowing and telling our stories.

SHARING YOUR STORY

What story have you been hesitant to share because it's a story of brokenness? What kind of healing needs to take place so that you can more fully know your story? The bottom line of all our stories is the transformation Christ brings to our lives. If ours is not a story of brokenness, then we haven't truly met Jesus. "But we have this treasure in jars of clay to show that this all-surpassing power is from God and not from us. We are hard pressed on every side, but not crushed; perplexed, but not in despair; persecuted, but not abandoned; struck down, but not destroyed. We always carry around in our body the death of Jesus, so that the life of Jesus may also be revealed in our body" (2 Corinthians 4:7 – 10). We are nothing but fragile vessels, full of cracks, and yet the perfect kind of vessel to let the light of Christ shine through. Do you believe that even though you are broken, God can actually heal you and make you into a beautiful vessel to display his glory? Do you believe that he can give you wisdom and influence and opportunities to speak life into others through the story he is writing in you? He will do that for you if you ask him.

We all have the opportunity to influence others with our stories. In some ways it's what hymn writer Katherine Hankey calls an "old, old story of Jesus and his love." In other ways it's as unique as a personal fingerprint, as evidenced by the way God works in the individual heart. I will have opportunities to share my story with people who will need to hear how Christ has worked in my life. You will have opportunity to share your story with people I'll never meet, or whom my story wouldn't impact at all. But before you can share your story, you need to have a story to share. What's yours? Part of the blind man's story was, "I was blind but now I see." You fill in the blanks: "I was _____ but now I'm _____." What story of hope and healing is God writing in your life?

Finding freedom from the secrets we keep is a lifelong journey. My story isn't finished yet, but I have total confidence that the great God of the universe has some amazing chapters still to write. Chapters filled with hopes and dreams, fears and failures, with the end result bringing glory to him if I don't muddy the waters. I rest in the confidence "that he who began a good work in [us] will carry it on to completion until the day of Christ Jesus" (Philippians 1:6).

DISCUSSION QUESTIONS

1. What is your deepest point of brokenness? If you can, share it with the group or a trusted friend.

2. Do you sense God is working with you to bring you to wholeness? How is he doing that?

3. How have you struggled with your view of God?

4. Take some time to reread John 9:1–25 and grapple with the ways you would fill in the blanks. "I was blind but now I see!" I was _____, but now I'm _____.

5. Spiritual friendship is one of the ways God moves us toward wholeness. If you aren't in a close relationship with another woman, would you commit to developing a deepening friendship? How will you go about doing this?

6. I hope some of my story has sparked some personal memories in you. Take some time to journal about your own story and then share pieces of your story with a friend. When we share our stories, we build up our faith.

ACKNOWLEDGMENTS

When I began this project, I had no idea how many people I would need to thank. Forget that it takes a village to raise a child. It takes villages, countries, and beyond to write a book. Okay, maybe that's a bit overstated, but these people whom I'm so thankful for have contributed in ways I can't put into words.

First of all to the *Midday Connection* listeners who have journeyed miles with me. They have shared their lives and their stories, and I will never be the same.

My Redbud Writers' Guild group has been invaluable in this process. They are Tracey Bianchi, Suanne Camfield, Jennifer Grant, Keri Wyatt Kent, Helen Lee, Shayne Moore, Caryn Rivadeneira, Melinda Schmidt, Karen Halvorsen Schreck, Arloa Sutter, Angie Weszely, and Princess Kasune Zulu. They are a prolific writers' group. Google their names to find some of their already published works.

Dear friends encouraged me to keep going when I was deeply discouraged in the midst of the process—friends like Sandy Towers, Angie Thomas, Nancy Kane, Faith Lee, and Joe Carlson.

This book wouldn't exist without the work of my agent, Chris Ferebee, the constant encouragement of Margaret Feinberg and Leif Oines, and the skillful work of editors Evelyn Bence and Sandy Vander Zicht.

I'm thankful to some women of wisdom who have cheered me on for a number of years. I deeply value these relationships. Thank you to Dee Brestin, Janet Davis, Jan Silvious, and Christine Wyrtzen.

Family, in my case, has been a constant encouragement. My mom and dad are *amazing* people! Their "open heart, open home" posture has shaped who I am. They are probably my biggest cheerleaders. My brothers, Denis and David, have also been loving supporters, and I can't forget my "favorite" cousin, James Watson, and his wife, Rondise, who are more like siblings than cousins.

Some of my more emotional supporters live under the same roof with me. My son, John, asked me not to write the final word in the manuscript until he was present. As I typed that word, he launched into a prayer I'll never forget, asking God to "bless what Mom wrote, and help a lot of women with the words of this book." It brought this mom to tears.

My husband, Mike, is not only a great idea guy and title picker, but he believes in me many times over when my self-belief is waning. He is chief among my supporters. I love him dearly, and the past five-plus years have been my happiest.

When I saw the faith I'd proclaimed become the faith I owned, I knew the ultimate thanks had to go to Christ himself. Jesus stepped into the mess of my life and walked each wearying step with me, stopping often to wash my feet. He is my light, my strength, and my salvation.

FOR FURTHER
READING

CHAPTER ONE: IT'S LONELY AT CHURCH

Brestin, Dee. *The God of All Comfort.*

Cloud, Henry, and John Townsend. *Making Small Groups Work.*

———. *Safe People.*

Dawn, Marva J. *My Soul Waits: Solace for the Lonely in the Psalms.*

Elliot, Elisabeth. *The Path of Loneliness.*

Frank, Anne. *The Diary of a Young Girl.*

Gire, Ken. *Windows of the Soul.*

Gresh, Dannah. *The Secret of the Lord.*

Sanders, J. Oswald. *Facing Loneliness.*

FICTION

Brontë, Charlotte. *Jane Eyre.*

**CHAPTER TWO: BEST FRIENDS FOREVER —
OR MAYBE NOT**

Brestin, Dee. *The Friendships of Women.*

Cloud, Henry, and John Townsend. *Boundaries.*

———. *Safe People.*

Crabb, Larry. *Soul Talk.*

Davis, Janet. *The Feminine Soul.*

Kane, Ray and Nancy. *From Fear to Love.*

Petherbridge, Laura. *When "I Do" Becomes "I Don't."*
Silvious, Jan. *Fool-Proofing Your Life.*
———. *Please Don't Say You Need Me.*
Smalley, Erin, and Carrie Oliver. *Grown-up Girlfriends.*
Wilson, Sandra D. *Hurt People Hurt People.*
———. *Released from Shame.*

FICTION

Baum, Frank. *The Wizard of Oz.*
Brontë, Charlotte. *Jane Eyre.*
White, E. B. *Charlotte's Web.*

CHAPTER THREE: DREAMING —
AND WEEPING — FOR OUR CHILDREN

Clarkson, Sally. *The Mission of Motherhood: Touching Your Child's Heart for Eternity.*
Goyer, Tricia. *Life Interrupted.*
Kimmel, Tim. *Grace-Based Parenting.*
Koonce, Katherine. *Parenting the Way God Parents: Refusing to Recycle Your Parents' Mistakes.*
Moore, Walker. *Rite of Passage Parenting.*
Perry, Linda Ellen, and Lynellen D. S. Perry. *How to Survive Your Teen's Pregnancy.*
Schooler, Jayne E. *Mom, Dad ... I'm Pregnant.*

FICTION

Hawthorne, Nathaniel. *The Scarlet Letter.*
Wright, Vinita Hampton. *The Winter Seeking.*

WEBSITE

Teen Mother Choices International, www.tmcint.org

CHAPTER FOUR: YOU'D BETTER WATCH OUT

Adams, Carol J. *Woman Battering.*
Berry, Dawn Bradley. *The Domestic Violence Sourcebook.*
Canfield, Muriel. *Broken and Battered.*
Coates, Jan. *Set Free.*
Engel, Beverly. *The Emotionally Abused Woman.*
Evans, Patricia. *The Verbally Abusive Relationship.*
———. *Controlling People.*
Hegstrom, Paul. *Angry Men and the Women Who Love Them.*
Kroeger, Catherine Clark, and Nancy Nason-Clark. *No Place for Abuse.*
Miles, Al. *Domestic Violence: What Every Pastor Needs to Know.*
Miller, Mary Susan. *No Visible Wounds.*
Nason-Clark, Nancy. *The Battered Wife.*
———and Catherine Clark Kroeger. *Refuge from Abuse.*
Rinck, Margaret J. *Christian Men Who Hate Women.*
Scott, Sandra. *Charmers and Con Artists.*
Silvious, Jan. *Fool-Proofing Your Life.*
Stewart, Donald. *Refuge: A Pathway Out of Domestic Violence and Abuse.*
Vernick, Leslie. *The Emotionally Destructive Relationship.*

FICTION

Brontë, Anne. *The Tenant of Wildfell Hall.*
Wright, Vinita Hampton. *Velma Still Cooks in Leeway.*

WEBSITES

www.focusministries1.org
http://www.focusministries1.org/SafetyPlan.pdf (specifics of developing a safety plan)
www.ndvh.org or National Domestic Violence Hotline, 1-800-799-SAFE

CHAPTER FIVE: NEVER ENOUGH

Arterburn, Stephen, and Fred and Brenda Stoeker. *Every Heart Restored.*

———. *Every Man's Battle.*

Carnes, Patrick. *Out of the Shadows.*

Cloud, Henry, and John Townsend. *Boundaries.*

———. *Boundaries Face to Face: How to Have That Difficult Conversation You've Been Avoiding.*

Laaser, Debra. *Shattered Vows.*

Laaser, Mark R. *Faithful and True.*

Leahy, Michael. *Porn Nation.*

Means, Marsha. *Living with Your Husband's Secret Wars.*

Means, Patrick. *Men's Secret Wars.*

Tauke, Beverly Hubble. *Healing Your Family Tree.*

VanVonderen, Jeff, Dale Ryan, and Juanita Ryan. *Soul Repair.*

Wilson, Meg. *Hope after Betrayal.*

FICTION

Stevenson, Robert Louis. *Dr. Jekyll and Mr. Hyde.*

Wilde, Oscar. *The Picture of Dorian Gray.*

WEBSITES

Somebody's Daughter: A Journey to Freedom from Pornography (audio project), www.musicforthesoul.org

Internet blocking software: www.bsecure.com, www.covenant eyes.com, www.internetsafety.com

CHAPTER SIX: SINGLE WITH CHILDREN

Aldrich, Sandra P. *From One Single Mother to Another.*

Armstrong, Brenda. *Financial Relief for Single Parents.*

Frisbie, David, and Lisa Frisbie. *Raising Great Kids on Your Own.*

Leman, Kevin. *Single Parenting That Works.*

Richmond, Gary. *Successful Single Parenting.*
Thomas, Angela. *My Single Mom Life.*

FICTION

Olsen, Tillie. "I Stand Here Ironing" from *Tell Me a Riddle.*

CHAPTER SEVEN: BLESS THE BROKEN ROAD

ON DIVORCE

Carter, Les. *Grace and Divorce.*
Frisbie, David, and Lisa Frisbie. *Moving Forward after Divorce.*
Petherbridge, Laura. *When "I Do" Becomes "I Don't."*
———. *When Your Marriage Dies.*
Smoke, Jim. *Growing through Divorce.*

ON REMARRIAGE

Frisbie, David, and Lisa Frisbie. *Happily Remarried.*
House, H. Wayne. *Divorce and Remarriage: Four Christian Views.*
Instone-Brewer, David. *Divorce and Remarriage in the Church.*
Keener, Craig. *And Marries Another.*
Kolbaba, Ginger. *Surprised by Remarriage.*
Leman, Kevin. *Step-Parenting 101.*
Marsolini, Maxine. *Raising Children in Blended Families.*
Parrott, Les and Leslie. *Saving Your Second Marriage Before It Starts.*
Petherbridge, Laura, and Ron Deal. *The Smart Stepmom.*
Strauss, Mark L. *Remarriage after Divorce in Today's Church.*
Tauber, Edward M., and Jim Smoke. *Finding the Right One after Divorce.*

CHAPTER EIGHT: BARBIE LIVES ON

Ashcroft, Mary Ellen. *Temptations Women Face.*

Barger, Lilian Calles. *Eve's Revenge.*

Eckert, Kim Gaines. *Stronger Than You Think.*

Graham, Michelle. *Wanting to Be Her.*

Gresh, Dannah. *Secret Keeper: The Delicate Power of Modesty.*

Hersh, Sharon. *Mom, I Feel Fat.*

Mintle, Dr. Linda. *Making Peace with Your Thighs.*

Newman, Deborah. *Comfortable in Your Own Skin.*

Webb, Heather. *Redeeming Eve.*

FICTION

Pierce, Bethany. *Feeling for Bones.*

CHAPTER NINE: I LOVE TO TELL THE STORY

Allender, Dan. *To Be Told: Know Your Story, Shape Your Future.*

Crabb, Larry. *The Pressure's Off: There's a New Way to Live.*

Davis, Janet. *The Feminine Soul.*

Gire, Ken. *Windows of the Soul.*

Harling, Becky. *Rewriting Your Emotional Script.*

James, Carolyn Custis. *When Life and Beliefs Collide.*

Kraft, Alan. *Good News for Those Trying Harder.*

Tauke, Beverly Hubble. *Healing Your Family Tree.*

Tournier, Paul. *The Gift of Feeling.*

Wilson, Sandra D. *Released from Shame: Moving Beyond the Pain of the Past.*

Wright, Vinita Hampton. *Days of Deepening Friendship.*

FICTION

Berry, Wendell. *Jayber Crow.*

Groot, Tracy. *Madman.*

Paton, Alan. *Cry the Beloved Country.*

———. *Too Late the Phalarope.*

Robinson, Marilynne. *Housekeeping.*

NOTES

CHAPTER ONE: IT'S LONELY AT CHURCH

1. Dannah Gresh, *The Secret of the Lord* (Nashville: Thomas Nelson, 2005), xxii.
2. Henry Cloud and John Townsend, *Safe People* (Grand Rapids: Zondervan, 1995).
3. C. S. Lewis, *Mere Christianity* (New York: Macmillan, 1952), 163.

**CHAPTER TWO: BEST FRIENDS FOREVER —
OR MAYBE NOT**

1. Oswald Chambers, *My Utmost for His Highest* (New York: Dodd, Mead, 1935), 224 (entry for August 11).
2. Frederick Buechner, *Whistling in the Dark* (San Francisco: HarperOne, 1993), 117.

**CHAPTER THREE: DREAMING —
AND WEEPING — FOR OUR CHILDREN**

1. Caroline Langston, "Facing the Truth," Good Letters blog of *Image Journal* (November 2, 2009), http://imagejournal.org/page/blog/facing-the-truth.

CHAPTER FOUR: YOU'D BETTER WATCH OUT

1. Carolyn Custis James, *Lost Women of the Bible* (Grand Rapids: Zondervan, 2005), 95.
2. Janet Davis, *The Feminine Soul* (Colorado Springs: NavPress, 2006), 13.

3. William Barclay, *The Gospel of John*, vol. 2 (Edinburgh: St. Andrews Press, 1955), 3.

4. Erwin Lutzer and Rebecca Lutzer, *Jesus, Lover of a Woman's Soul* (Wheaton, Ill.: Tyndale House, 2006), 105.

5. Ibid., 106.

6. The authorized English Version of the Qur'an, Sura 4:34.

7. Craig Keener, "Some Biblical Reflections on Justice, Rape, and an Insensitive Society," in *Women, Abuse, and the Bible: How Scripture Can Be Used to Hurt or Heal*, ed. Catherine Clark Kroeger and James R. Beck (Grand Rapids: Baker, 1996), 121.

CHAPTER FIVE: NEVER ENOUGH

1. Christine J. Gardner, "Tangled in the Worst of the Web," *Christianity Today* 45, no. 4 (March 5, 2001).

2. John LaRue, "Christians and Sex Survey," *Leadership Journal* (March 2005).

3. Jill Savage, *Is There Really Sex after Kids?* (Grand Rapids: Zondervan, 2003), 59.

4. From *Out of the Shadows: Understanding Sexual Addiction*, 3rd ed., by Patrick Carnes, PhD. Copyright 1983, 1992, 2001 by Hazelden Foundation. Reprinted by permission of Hazelden Foundation, Center City, MN.

5. Ibid.

6. Dr. Henry Cloud, Dr. John Townsend, *Boundaries Face to Face* (Grand Rapids: Zondervan, 2003), 17.

CHAPTER SIX: SINGLE WITH CHILDREN

1. Adele Calhoun, *Spiritual Disciplines Handbook* (Westmont, Ill.: InterVarsity, 2005), 52.

2. Nancy Fuchs-Kreimer, "A Jewish Exploration: Widows, Orphans, and Charity-as-Justice," *Cathedral Age* (Fall 2006), 18.

CHAPTER SEVEN: BLESS THE BROKEN ROAD

1. Warren Wiersbe, *The Bible Exposition Commentary*, vol. I (Colorado Springs: Victor, 1989), 83.
2. Matthew Henry, *Matthew Henry's Concise Commentary on the Bible*, www.biblegateway.com/resources/commentaries/ Matthew-Henry/Matt/Guilt-Jerusalem.
3. Mary A. Bullis, *The Miraculous Journey* (Ventura, Calif.: Regal, 2004), 122–23.
4. "New Marriage and Divorce Statistics Released," www.barna. org/barna-update/article/15-familykids/42-new-marriage-and-divorce-statistics-released.
5. Erwin Lutzer and Rebecca Lutzer, *Jesus, Lover of a Woman's Soul* (Wheaton, Ill.: Tyndale House, 2006), 39–40.
6. Jan L. Richardson, *Night Visions* (Cleveland: Pilgrim Press, 1998), 111.

CHAPTER EIGHT: BARBIE LIVES ON

1. www.dove.us/#/cfrb/girlsonly/body_facts.aspx/.
2. Quiz taken from Michelle Graham, *Wanting to Be Her: Body Image Secrets Victoria Won't Tell You*. Copyright © 2005 by Michelle Graham. Used by permission of InterVarsity Press, PO Box 1400, Downers Grove, IL 60515. www.ivpress.com.
3. Sheila Walsh, *Bring Back the Joy* (Grand Rapids: Zondervan, 1998), 76.
4. Ibid., 89.
5. Carolyn Custis James, *Lost Women of the Bible* (Grand Rapids: Zondervan, 2005) 153.
6. Ibid., 154.

CHAPTER NINE: I LOVE TO TELL THE STORY

1. Alan Kraft, *Good News for Those Trying Harder* (Colorado Springs: Cook, 2008), 32–33.

2. Ibid., 31.

3. Vinita Hampton Wright, *The Soul Tells a Story* (Westmont, Ill.: InterVarsity, 2005), 168.

4. Luci Shaw, *Breath for the Bones* (Nashville: Thomas Nelson, 2007), 57.

5. Lilias Trotter, *A Blossom in the Desert* (Grand Rapids: Discovery House, 2007), 115. Originally from Trotter's journal, August 8, 1899.

STAY IN TOUCH!

You've heard my story; I'd love to hear yours. Shoot me an email at anita@anitalustrea.com.

Please visit my website too: www.anitalustrea.com. You can join the discussion on my blog and check out the other information on my website, including my speaking schedule. Maybe I'll be coming to your city.

If you'd like to have me come speak at your church conference or retreat, email me at anita@anitalustrea.com. I speak on a variety of topics including the issues talked about in *What Women Tell Me*.

If you're unfamiliar with the radio show I host, I hope you'll check out our website at www.middayconnection.org. You can either listen to us on your local Christian radio station (find station listings on the *Midday Connection* website), stream the program live from our website at noon central time, or download *Midday Connection* as a podcast. We talk about issues that are relevant in the lives of women, like the topics covered in *What Women Tell Me*.

ABOUT THE AUTHOR

ANITA LUSTREA IS A WOMAN ON a mission to communicate freedom to women. She is wife to Mike Murphy, a pastor at Christ Church of Oak Brook, and Director of Spiritual Transformation at Breakthrough Ministries on the west side of Chicago. Mike makes Anita laugh and is the anchor in her life. Her son, John, is one of the brightest spots in her world. He is soon to be a high school graduate planning to major in history in college.

Anita has worked for Moody Radio for twenty-six years now, the last eleven hosting *Midday Connection*. She thanks God for the opportunity to learn and grow through *Midday* along with a whole community of women from across the country.

Besides authoring *What Women Tell Me*, Anita helped edit *Daily Seeds from Women Who Walk in Faith*, and *Come to Our Table*.

Anita is part of Redbud Writer's Guild, a prolific writer's group full of gifted women writing for the kingdom of God.

Anita is originally from Maine, the most beautiful state in the Union according to her! If she can't be in Maine, her second choice is right where she is, in Chicago. Reading, writing, bird watching, and drinking hot tea are some of her favorite pastimes.

Midday Connection

Where you turn for . . .

relationships
laughter
a good book
Bible study
encouragement
cooking ideas
financial advice
health tips
and...

all the little things that make a big difference in your day.

Midday Connection

A community
of women
growing together

Noon, Central Time
on Moody Radio
www.middayconnection.org

Lori Neff, Melinda Schmidt, and Anita Lustrea

Share Your Thoughts

With the Author: Your comments will be forwarded to the author when you send them to *zauthor@zondervan.com*.

With Zondervan: Submit your review of this book by writing to *zreview@zondervan.com*.

Free Online Resources at
www.zondervan.com

Zondervan AuthorTracker: Be notified whenever your favorite authors publish new books, go on tour, or post an update about what's happening in their lives at www.zondervan.com/authortracker.

Daily Bible Verses and Devotions: Enrich your life with daily Bible verses or devotions that help you start every morning focused on God. Visit www.zondervan.com/newsletters.

Free Email Publications: Sign up for newsletters on Christian living, academic resources, church ministry, fiction, children's resources, and more. Visit www.zondervan.com/newsletters.

Zondervan Bible Search: Find and compare Bible passages in a variety of translations at www.zondervanbiblesearch.com.

Other Benefits: Register yourself to receive online benefits like coupons and special offers, or to participate in research.